THE PRIVATE LIVES OF THE
TUDOR MONARCHS

1. *The very image of a Tudor monarch – Henry VIII at the height of his powers. Perhaps the grandest of all Holbein's State portraits.*

THE
PRIVATE LIVES
OF THE
TUDOR MONARCHS

Selected and edited by
CHRISTOPHER FALKUS

London
The Folio Society
1974

PRINTED IN GREAT BRITAIN
Printed and bound by Jarrold & Sons Limited, Norwich
Set in 'Monophoto' Poliphilus 12 point leaded 1 point

1

CONTENTS

PREFACE   7

HENRY VII

Henry to Margaret Beaufort, 1501   11
Anecdote of the death of Prince Arthur   12
The Court Festivals of Henry VII   14

HENRY VIII

Henry to Erasmus, 1507   18
Henry to Ferdinand of Aragon, 1509   20
Henry to Anne Boleyn, 1527–8   21
Hall's *Chronicle*   34
    The Twenty-eighth Year, 1536–7   34
    The Twenty-ninth Year, 1537–8   36
    The Thirty-first Year, 1539–40   37
Henry to Katherine Parr, 1544   46
Song: 'Pastance with good Company'   51

EDWARD VI

Edward's *Chronicle*   53

JANE GREY

From *The Schoolmaster* by Roger Ascham   75
From *A Harbour for Faithful Subjects* by John Aylmer   76

MARY TUDOR

Mary to Henry VIII, 1533   79
Eustace Chapuys to Charles V, 1534   80

'Concerning the Child-bed of Queen Mary' from Foxe's   81
    Book of Martyrs
Giovanni Michele, 1557   84
Extract from Mary's Last Will and Testament   84

QUEEN ELIZABETH

Lady Bryan to Thomas Cromwell, 1536   88
Elizabeth to Katherine Parr, 1544   91
Elizabeth to Edward VI, 1550   91
Elizabeth to Queen Mary, 1554   92
From *The Schoolmaster* by Roger Ascham   96
Elizabeth to Eric, King of Sweden, 1560   98
Encounter with the Dean of St Paul's, 1561   100
Melville at the English Court, 1564   102
Elizabeth to Mary, Queen of Scots, 1567   107
Elizabeth to George Talbot, Earl of Shrewsbury, 1577   108
Elizabeth to Francis, Duke of Anjou, 1580   109
Elizabeth to Francis, Duke of Anjou, 1581   112
Elizabeth to Robert Dudley, Earl of Leicester, 1586   113
Elizabeth to Mary, Queen of Scots, 1586   115
Elizabeth to James VI of Scotland, 1587   115
Elizabeth to Robert Devereux, Earl of Essex, 1596   117
Elizabeth to Lady Norris, 1597   117
Mr Fenton to Sir John Harington, 1597   119
Sir John Harington to Sir Hugh Portman, 1601   120
Sir John Harington to his wife, 1602   122
Sir John Harington to Mr Robert Markham, 1606   123

ACKNOWLEDGEMENTS   128

PREFACE

As with all monarchs who rule as well as reign, the gap between the public and private lives of the Tudors is a narrow one. The marriages of Henry VIII and the courtships of Elizabeth were affairs of state; just as the business of government was, in part, a matter of the sovereign's domestic routine.

In another sense the Tudors had virtually no private life at all, for privacy itself was a very rare commodity at Court. From morning until night – and through the night – they were almost never alone, accompanied as they were by servants, ladies- or gentlemen-in-waiting, courtiers, officials, favourites, place-seekers.

Yet it is precisely this merging of the public and private which gives a special significance to an understanding of the monarchs as personalities, for their characters, temperaments, tastes, qualities, defects, accomplishments, must be viewed in the context of an intensely personal style of government.

The selection of documents presented here is intended to reflect some of these aspects, and to illustrate from contemporary material the less formal side of Tudor kingship.

2. The succession of Henry VIII, from Sudeley Castle. A fine example of the political allegory, popular with the Tudors, this painting shows Mary and Philip, followed by Mars and the gods of war, contrasted with Elizabeth followed by Flora and the fruits of prosperity.

ILLUSTRATIONS

1.	Henry VIII at the height of his powers	*frontispiece*
2.	Succession of Henry VIII	*page* 7
3.	Henry VII in 1505	10
4.	Margaret Beaufort, Henry VII's mother	10
5.	Prince Arthur, eldest son of Henry VII	13
6.	Court entertainments and festivals of the period	14
7.	Henry VII's countersigned accounts	17
8.	Erasmus of Rotterdam	19
9, 10.	Henry VIII's armour	20
11.	Catherine of Aragon	23
12.	Anne Boleyn	23
13.	Henry VIII dining in the Privy Chamber	24
14.	Henry VIII by Horenbout, in 1535	26
15.	Court dress of the Tudor period	29
16.	An early portrait of Anne Boleyn	31
17.	Design by Holbein for a chimney-piece	32
18.	The King's Lock	33
19.	Henry VIII and his family	34–5
20.	Hampton Court by Wyngaerde	36
21.	Jane Seymour	37
22.	Jane Seymour's drinking cup	37
23.	Anne of Cleves	39
24.	Henry VIII's astrolabe	40
25.	Design for a pendant by Holbein	43
26.	A miniature thought to be Catherine Howard	44
27.	Henry VIII in old age, with his jester	47
28.	Katherine Parr	47
29.	Henry VIII's writing-desk	48
30.	A song by Henry VIII, probably in his own hand	50
31.	Edward VI as a child, by Holbein	52
32.	Edward Seymour, Duke of Somerset	53
33.	The coronation procession of Edward VI	54–5
34.	A tilt match in progress	56
35.	A woodcut illustration from an early history	57
36.	A political allegory showing Edward VI confounding the Pope	58

37. A merchant ship of the period by Holbein   61
38. A contemporary view of Calais   62
39. The country round Westminster Palace in the 1550s   64
40. State portrait of Edward as King   66
41. A section of a panorama of London by Wyngaerde   68
42. State portrait of Lady Jane Grey   74
43. A triptych summary of Lady Jane Grey's nine-day reign   77
44. Mary Tudor   78
45. Mary Tudor and Philip II of Spain   82
46. Mary as Queen   85
47. The young Elizabeth   86
48. Queen Elizabeth leading a Court dance   87
49. Elizabeth's dedication to Katherine Parr   89
50. A late portrait of Katherine Parr   90
51. Letter to Mary in Elizabeth's own hand   93, 94
52. Queen Elizabeth's virginals   97
53. Eric of Sweden   99
54. Nowell, Dean of St Paul's   101
55. A portrait by Zuccaro of Queen Elizabeth   102
56. The Earl of Leicester from a miniature by Hilliard   103
57. Queen Elizabeth giving audience to two Dutch ambassadors   104
58. Queen Elizabeth's table clock   105
59. Queen Elizabeth   106
60. Mary Stuart, Queen of Scotland   107
61. Nonsuch Palace, destroyed in 1670   109
62. Francis, Duke of Anjou and Duke of Alençon   111
63. A political allegory, 1579   114
64. The execution of Mary, Queen of Scots   115
65. James VI of Scotland   116
66. The Earl of Essex   118
67. Sir John Harington, Elizabeth's godson   121
68. Sketch of Queen Elizabeth's funeral cortège   126-7

3. *Henry VII in 1505, painting by an
unknown artist.*

4. *Margaret Beaufort, Henry VII's
mother: a painting in St John's College,
one of her Cambridge foundations.*

HENRY VII

Henry VII, founder of the Tudor dynasty, was born in 1457, the son of Edmund Tudor, Earl of Richmond, and of Margaret Beaufort, a descendant of Edward III through John of Gaunt. After Henry's victory over Richard III at Bosworth in 1485 he was able to unite the Houses of York and Lancaster through his marriage to Elizabeth of York and eventually to bring about a period of political stability and financial prosperity.

Little survives to tell us about Henry's personality. Of all the Tudors he remains perhaps the most obscure. Contemporaries recognized his 'vast ability' and he was certainly conscientious, methodical and shrewd. But he lacked the flamboyance and extravagance associated with other sovereigns of his age and, not surprisingly, he was widely regarded as a miser in his approach to the royal finances. Such a king could be respected, but never popular.

As a king, Henry was outstandingly successful. His rule saw the once-bankrupt monarchy rise not merely to solvency but to wealth; he restored law and order to a disordered kingdom; above all he overcame the challenges of a number of rival claimants to the throne so that, ultimately, he was able to reign in peace over a united country. He was a devoted son and husband, but his last years were increasingly lonely and unhappy – particularly after the death of his eldest son Arthur in 1502 and of his wife in 1503– and the nation began to look forward eagerly to the changes which would come with his successor, the vigorous and spendthrift Henry VIII, who was to prove in almost every way such a contrast to his father.

Henry to Margaret Beaufort, ? July 1501

Few letters from Henry to his mother survive, but one, written in his own hand, demonstrates both his affection towards her and a growing awareness of his own failing powers. Having granted her the dispensation necessary for one of her Cambridge foundations, he wrote:

. . . all of which things according to your desire and pleasure, I have, with all my heart and good will given and granted unto you; and my dame, not only in this but in all other things that I know should be to your honour and pleasure, and weal of your soul, I shall be glad to please you as your heart can desire it, and I know well, that I am as much bounden so to do, as any creature living for the great and singular motherly love and affection that it hath pleased you at all times to bear me. Wherefore, mine own most loving mother, in my most hearty manner I thank you, beseeching you of your good continuance in the same.

Madame, I have encumbered you now with this my long writing, but methinks that I can do no less, considering that it is so seldom that I do write, wherefore I beseech you to pardon me, for verily, madame, my sight is nothing so perfect as it has been, and I know well it will appear daily wherefore I trust that you will not be displeased, though I write not so often with mine own hand, for on my faith I have been three days ere I could make an end of this letter.

Anecdote of the death of Prince Arthur

The following story from an unknown source tells of the grief of the royal couple on the news of the death of their eldest son. It was first printed in Leland's De Rebus Brittanicus Collectanea *(1715) – and most recently in* Henry VII *by S. B. Chrimes.*

In the year of our Lord God 1502, the second day of April, in the Castle of Ludlow deceased Prince Arthur first begotten son of our Sovereign Lord King Henry the VIIth and in the 17th year of his reign. Immediately after his death Sir Richard Poole his Chamberlain, with others of his Council, wrote and sent letters to the king and Council to Greenwich, where his grace and the queen lay, and certified them of the prince's departure. The which Council discreetly sent for the king's ghostly Father a friar observant, to whom they showed this most sorrowful and heavy tidings, and desired him in his best manner to show it to the king. He in the morning of the Tuesday following, somewhat before the time accustomed, knocked at the King's Chamber door, and when the king understood it was his confessor, he commanded to let him in. The confessor then commanded all those present to avoid, and after due salutation . . . showed his grace, that his dearest son was departed to God. When his grace understood that sorrowful heavy tidings, he sent for the queen, saying that he and his queen would take

5. Prince Arthur, eldest son of Henry VII, whose early death in 1502 was to bring his brother to the throne as Henry VIII.

the painful sorrows together. After that she was come and saw the king her lord, and that natural and painful sorrow, as I have heard say, she with full great and constant comfortable words besought his grace that he would first after God remember the weal of his own noble person, the comfort of his realm and of her. She then said that my lady his mother had never no more children but him only, and that God by His grace had ever preserved him, and brought him where he was. Over that, how that God had left him yet a fair prince, two fair princesses, that God is where he was, and we are both young enough. And that the prudence and wisdom of his grace spread over all Christendom, so that it should please him to take this accordingly thereunto. Then the king thanked her of her good comfort. After that she departed and came to her own chamber, natural and motherly remembrance of that great loss smote her so sorrowful to the heart that those about her were feign to send for the king to comfort her. Then his grace of true gentle and faithful love, in good haste came and relieved her, and showed her how wise counsel she had given him before, and he for his part would thank God for his son, and would she should do in like wise.

6. *Court entertainments and festivals of the period: such extravagant display was character-istic of Renaissance monarchs.*

The Court Festivals of Henry VII

These are some extracts from the careful records kept by John Heron, the king's treasurer. They show that Henry was perfectly capable of enjoying himself; that he knew the value of royal display; but that every item was carefully accounted for under his business-like régime.

PAYMENTS RELATING TO COURT ENTERTAINMENTS

1492

Jan. 1st.	Item to my Lord of Oxon. players in reward . . .	20s
	Item to my Lord Privy Seal fool in reward	10s
Jan. 5th.	Item to two Swiss great tabarers	40s
Jan. 8th.	Item to the king to play at cards	100s
Jan. 16th.	Item to one that brought the king a lion in reward .	53s 4d
Jan. 24th.	Item to Jakes Haute for diverse necessaries bought for the king as tables, cheese, glasses and other .	56s 6d
Jan. 29th.	Item to my Lady York minstrels in reward	20s

Feb. 12th.	Item to Pechie the fool in reward	6s 8d
Mar. 4th.	Item to the child that playeth on the records . . .	20s
	Item to my Lord of Suffolk's minstrels in reward .	13s 4d
Apr. 6th.	Item to Guillim for flutes with a case	70s
Apr. 29th.	Item to one that played on the lute in reward . .	6s 8d
May 7th.	At Shene. To the clerk of the works for making	
	of the lists at Shene	£24 2s 10d
May 8th.	Item for making a case for the king's steward and	
	a case for James Hide's harp	20s 8d
Jun. 4th.	Item to Sir Edward Borough which the king lost	
	at buttes with his crossbow	13s 4d
Jun. 10th.	Item to a Spaniard that played the fool	40s
Jun. 11th.	Item to one that played on the drone	6s 8d
Jun. 17th.	Item to Master Guyfford for spears, spearheads and	
	vamplats bought for the jousts	£9 6s
Jun. 18th.	Item to the foolish Duke of Lancaster	3s 4d
Jun. 30th.	Item to the king which he lost at cards	£40
Jul. 8th.	Item to the maidens of Lambeth for a May . . .	10s
Jul. 31st.	Item to the foolish Duke of Lancaster	6s 8d
	Item to the shamews of Madeston in reward . . .	6s 8d
	Item for an horse and saddle, bridle and spurs	
	bought for Dego, the Spanish fool	18s 6d
Aug. 1st.	Item to the children for singing in the garden . .	3s 4d
Sep. 24th.	Item to the minstrels of Sandwich in reward . .	10s
Oct. 2nd.	Item to the minstrels that played in the Swan . .	13s 4d
	Item to Dego, the Spanish fool, in reward . . .	4s 8d
Oct. 18th.	Item to the waytes of Canterbury	10s
	Item to the waytes of Dover	6s 8d
Oct. 24th.	Item to Ringeley, Abbot of Misreule	100s

1493

Jan. 6th.	Item to Newark for making of a song	20s
Jan. 7th.	Item to my Lord of Northumberland's players in reward	20s
Mar. 2nd.	Item to Master Bray for rewards to them that brought	
	cocks at Shrovetide at Westminster	20s
Mar. 10th.	Item for a pair of tables and dice bought . . .	16s
	Item to my Lord Privy Seal fool for a reward . .	6s 8d

Mar. 11th.	Item to Dego the fool in reward	10s
Mar. 22nd.	Item to the fool, the Duke of Lancaster	6s 8d
Apr. 30th.	Item to the waytes of Coventry in reward . . .	10s
	Item to the foolish Duke of Lancaster in reward .	6s 8d
May 13th.	Item to the waytes of Northampton in reward . .	8s 4d
May 16th.	Item to Pudesey Piper on the bagpipe	6s 8d
Jun. 23rd.	Item to the making of the bonfire on Midsummer Eve	10s
Aug. 25th.	Item to the young damsel that danceth	.£30
Sep. 24th.	Item to Pachye the fool for a reward	6s 8d
	Item to him that had his bull baited in reward . . .	10s
Nov. 3rd.	Item to John Flee for Dick's the fools rayment . . .	21s
Nov. 12th.	Item to one Cornish for a prophecy in reward . .	13s 4d
Nov. 16th.	Item to Walter Alwyn for the revells at Estermes	£13 6s 8d
Nov. 30th.	Item delivered to a merchant for a pair of organs .	.£30
Dec. 1st.	Item to Basset riding for the organ player of Lichfield	13s 4d
Dec. 7th.	Item to the King of France fool in reward	£4

1494

Jan. 1st.	Item to four players of Essex in reward	20s
	Item to the players of Winbone Minister. . . .	20s
Jan. 2nd.	Item for playing of the morris dance	40s
Jan. 6th.	Item for clothing mad Dick the fool . . .	35s 7d
	Item to the French players for a reward	20s
	Item to the king's players for a reward . . .	53s 4d
Jan. 15th.	Item to my Lord of Bedford tumbler in reward .	13s 4d
Jan. 22nd.	Item to the king for his loss at cards	40s
Feb. 15th.	Item to Walter Alwyn in full payment for the	
	disguising made at Christmas	.£14 14s 4d
Feb. 18th.	Item to my Lady Margaret's minstrels	10s
Apr. 2nd.	Item to the king's piper for a reward . . .	6s 8d
Apr. 5th.	At Dertford.	
	Item to the waytes of the town in reward . . .	3s 4d
May 29th.	Item to one that tumbled before the king . . .	20s
Jun. 1st.	Item to Peche for the disguising in reward . .	£26 14s
Jun. 10th.	Item to one that joculed before the king . . .	10s
Jun. 13th.	Item to a Spaniard the tennis player	.£4
Jun. 24th.	Item for making of the bonfire in reward . . .	10s

Jul. 6th.	Item to Hugh Denes for balls at the paune play . .	12d
Jul. 26th.	Item to the tennis player for balls	2s
Aug. 14th.	Item to Sir Charles Somerset for the king's loss at tennis to Sir Robert Curson with the balls . .	27s 8d
Aug. 20th.	Item to the king for playing at the cards . . .	60s
Oct. 31st.	Item to the challengers at the jousts . . . £66 13s 4d	
	Item to the defenders at the jousts . . . £66 13s 4d	
Nov. 14th.	Item to a Spaniard that tumbled	40s
Nov. 29th.	Item to Jakes Haute for the disguising £20	
	Item to my Lord Prince's luter in reward . . .	20s
Dec. 31st.	Item to three players of Wycombe in reward . .	13s 4d

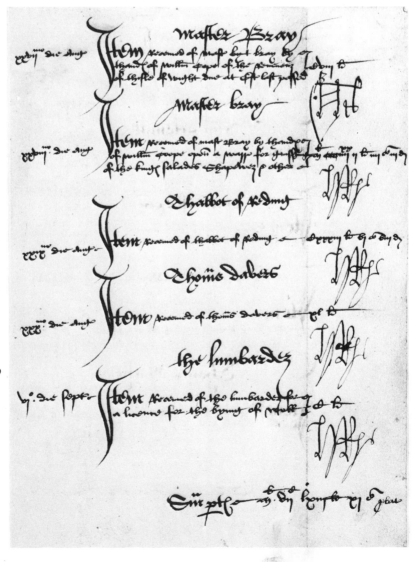

Henry VII's counter-
signature on each item of
the accounts underlines
the painstaking attention to
detail characteristic of this
most business-like of
monarchs.

HENRY VIII

In both his statesmanship and his private life Henry VIII showed himself arbitrary, strong-willed and ruthless. He pursued his political goals – the break with Rome, the Dissolution of the Monasteries – with the same remorseless dedication he showed in the pursuit of his private pleasures.

Endowed with enormous energy, Henry's early years were spent largely self-indulgently, hunting, jousting, feasting and in the company of his mistresses. But with time his health deteriorated until, near the end, his huge body, swollen with disease, had to be carried from place to place on a litter. Yet illness did not prevent him from exercising a very personal control over the government. Indeed, the personalities of few kings have so dominated affairs of state. The downfall of his three great servants – Wolsey, More and Cromwell – was at least partly due to their involvement in those dangerous areas where the king's public and private lives became entangled, while his marriages involved not merely the rise and fall of family factions at Court, but changes in the scope and direction of national policy.

Of all Tudor documents Henry's love-letters to Anne Boleyn are perhaps the most famous, and the most intimate. They are a remarkable series, showing both the sincerity of Henry's passion and the single-minded dedication with which he was prepared to sacrifice others – in this instance Catherine of Aragon and his daughter Mary – to his immediate object. It was a characteristic that was to be equally evident when the king tired of Anne herself.

Royal Supremacy was the keynote of his reign. In time Henry came to identify his interests and will with those of his country and of God, an assumption of personal authority which took him to a position of power in Church and State unequalled by any of his predecessors or successors in English history.

Henry to Erasmus, 17 January 1507

One of Henry's earliest surviving letters, this, written at the age of fifteen and two years before he became king, is remarkably precocious not because of its content but because of the striking self-confidence of a young boy seeking out the greatest scholar of the age as a correspondent.

Jesus is my hope.

I am greatly affected by your letter, most eloquent Erasmus, which is at once too elegant to be taken as written in haste, and at the same time too plain and simple to seem premeditated by a mind so ingenious. For in some way those epistles which by a mind thus endowed are brought forth with the more designed elaboration, in like manner carry with them a more studied difficulty. For while we apply ourselves to a purer eloquence, that a pert and clear manner of speech escapes us almost unawares. But this your epistle is to be esteemed as much for its evident perspicuity, so that, in fine, you seem to have achieved every point. But wherefore do I determine to laud your eloquence, whose renown is known throughout the whole world? Nothing that I am able to fashion in your praise can be enough worthy of that consummate erudition. Wherefore I pass over your praises, in which I think it the more fit to keep silence than to speak in manner too niggard.

The news of the death of the King of Castile my wholly and entirely and best-loved brother, I had reluctantly received very long before your letter. Would that the report thereof had either reached us much later or been less true! For never, since the death of my dearest mother, hath there come to me more hateful intelligence. And to speak truth, I was the scanter well-disposed towards your letter than its singular grace demanded, because it seemed to tear open again the wound to which time had brought insensibility. But indeed those things which are decreed by Heaven are so to be accepted by

Erasmus of Rotterdam, the celebrated Dutch scholar and humanist, who played a role in the developing attitudes of the time to Church and State.

mortal men. Continue, therefore, if in your parts there be any occurrents, to advertise us by letters, but may they be of happier sort. May God bring to a fortunate issue whatsoever may happen that is worthy to be remembered. Farewell.

From Richmond, the 17th day of January.

Henry to Ferdinand of Aragon, 1 November 1509

On 11 June 1509 Henry married Catherine of Aragon. Five months later he was writing to Ferdinand, his father-in-law, with the happy news of her pregnancy.

. . . Your daughter, her Serene Highness the Queen, our dearest consort, with the favour of heaven has conceived in her womb a living child, and is right heavy therewith, which we signify to your majesty for the great joy thereof that we take, and the exultation of our whole realm, and because it will be thus received by your majesty and her Serene Highness the Queen of Castile, to whom be pleased to give our hearty greeting. . . .

From our Palace of Greenwich, 1 November 1509.

Your good son,
HENRY R.

9, 10. Henry was a martial king, who accompanied his troops on several campaigns. However, his personal suits of armour, shown here, graphically illustrate the ravages of time on the royal figure.

Henry to Anne Boleyn

The famous series of love-letters to Anne Boleyn belong to the period 1527–8, though they cannot be placed in chronological order with complete certainty. By far the most intimate royal documents of the age, they foreshadow such great events as the fall of Wolsey, the struggle with Rome, Catherine's divorce and the Reformation itself.

I.

My Mistress and Friend,

I and my heart commit ourselves into your hands, beseeching you to hold us recommended to your good favour, and that your affection to us may not be by absence diminished; for great pity it were to increase our pain, seeing that absence makes enough of it, and indeed more than I could ever have thought, remembering us of a point in astronomy, which is this: that the longer the days are, the farther off is the sun, and yet, notwithstanding, the hotter; so is it with our love, for we by absence are far sundered, yet it nevertheless keeps its fervency, at the least on my part, holding in hope the like on yours; ensuring you that for myself the annoy of absence doth already too much vex me; and when I think upon the increase of that which of necessity I must needs suffer it is almost intolerable to me, were it not for the firm hope that I have of your ever-during affection towards me; and sometimes to put you in mind of this, and seeing that in person I cannot be in your presence, I send you now the thing most nearly thereto appertaining that it is possible to me to send, which is my picture set in a bracelet, with the whole device which already you know. Wishing myself in their place, when it should please you. This by the hand of your loyal servant and friend.

H.R.

2.

For so beautiful a gift, and so exceeding (taking it in all), I thank you right cordially; not alone for the fair diamond and the ship in which the solitary damsel is tossed about, but chiefly for the good intent and too-humble submission vouchsafed in this by your kindness; considering well that by occasion to merit it would not a little perplex me, if I were not aided therein by your great benevolence and goodwill, for the which I have sought, do seek, and shall always seek by all services to me possible there to remain, in the which my hope hath set up his everlasting rest, saying *aut illic aut nullibi.*

The proofs of your affection are such, the fine posies of the letters so warmly couched, that they constrain me ever truly to honour, love and serve you, praying that you will continue in this same firm and constant purpose, ensuring you, for my part, that I will the rather go beyond than make reciproque, if loyalty of heart, the desire to do you pleasure, even with my whole heart root, may serve to advance it.

Praying you also that if ever before I have in any way done you offence, that you will give me the same absolution that you ask, ensuring you that henceforth my heart shall be dedicate to you alone, greatly desirous that so my body could be as well, as God can bring to pass if it pleaseth Him, whom I entreat once each day for the accomplishment thereof, trusting that at length my prayer will be heard, wishing the time brief, and thinking it but long until we shall see each other again.

Written with the hand of that secretary who in heart, body and will is

Your loyal and most ensured servant,

H. autre (AB) ne cherce R.

3.

To my Mistress,

Because the time seems to me very long since I have heard of your good health and of you, the great affection that I bear you has prevailed with me to send this bearer to you, to be the better ascertained of your health and pleasure; and because since I parted with you I have been advised that the opinion in which I left you is now altogether changed, and that you will not come to Court, neither with my lady your mother, and if you could, nor yet any other way; the which report being true I cannot enough marvel at, seeing that I am well assured I have never since that time committed fault; and methinks it is but small recompense for the great love I bear you to keep me thus distanced both from the speech and the person of that she which of all the world I most do esteem; and if you love me with such settled affection as I trust, I assure me that this sundering of our two persons should be to you some small vexation, though in truth this doth not so much pertain to the mistress as to the servant.

Bethink you well, my mistress, that your absence doth not a little grieve me,

Catherine of Aragon, whose match with [Pri]nce Arthur and subsequent marriage to [He]nry VIII was to be largely instrumental in [the] events of the Reformation.

12. *Anne Boleyn, whose passionate love affair with Henry VIII was responsible for Catherine's downfall.*

13. *Henry VIII dining in the Privy Chamber: a drawing by Holbein.*

trusting that by your will it should not be so; but if I knew in truth that of your will you desired it, I could do none other than lament me of my ill fortune, abating by little and little my so great folly. And thus, for lack of time, I make an end of my rude letter, praying you to give credence to this bearer in that which he will tell you from me.

Written with the hand of your entire servant,
H.R.

4.

Debating with myself the contents of your letters, I have put myself in great distress, not knowing how to interpret them, whether to my disadvantage, as in some places is shown, or to advantage, as in others I understand them; praying you with all my heart that you will expressly certify me of your whole mind concerning the love between us two. For of necessity I must ensure me of this answer, having been now above one whole year struck with the dart of love, not being assured either of failure or of finding place in your heart and grounded affection. Which last point has kept me for some little time from calling you my mistress, since if you love me in some other sort save that of common affection that name in no wise belongs to you, for it denotes a singular love, far removed from the common. But if it shall please you to do me the office of a true, loyal mistress and friend, and to give yourself up, body and soul, to me who will be and have been your very loyal servant (if by your severity you do not forbid me), I promise you that not only shall the name be given you, but that also I will take you for my only mistress, rejecting from thought and affection all others save yourself, to serve you only. Beseeching you to make me answer absolute to this my rude letter, how far and in what I may put trust; and if it does not please you to make me answer by writing, assign me some place where I may have it from your own mouth, and with well-willing heart I will be there. No more, for fear of wearing you. Written with the hand of him who would willingly remain your

H.R.

5.

Although, my mistress, it hath not pleased you to remember the promise that you made me when I was last with you, which was to hear good news of you, and to have answer to my last letter; nevertheless, methinks it is the part of a true servant (seeing that otherwise he can hear nothing) to send to understand of the health of his mistress, and so, to acquit myself of the office of a true servant, I send you this letter, praying you to advertise me of your well-being, the which I pray God may endure as long as I would mine own. And to the intent that you may the more often remember me, I send you by this bearer a buck, killed by my hand late yesternight, trusting that as you eat of it you will have in mind the hunter. And thus, for lack of space, I will make an end of my letter. Written with the hand of your servant, who oft and again wisheth you in your brother's room.

H.R.

6.

Although it doth not appertain to a gentleman to take his lady in place of servant, nevertheless, in compliance with your desires, I willingly grant it to you, if thereby you can find yourself less unthankfully bestowed in the place by you chosen, than you have been in the place given by me. Thanking you right heartily for that it pleaseth you still to hold me in some remembrance.

Henry R.

14. Henry VIII by Horenbout, in 1535: a miniature in the Fitzwilliam Museum, Cambridge.

7.

The drawing near of that time which has for me been so long deferred so much rejoiceth me that it is as if it were already come. Nevertheless, the perfect accomplishing thereof cannot be until the two persons are together met, the which meeting is on my part the more desired than any earthly thing; for what joy in this world can be greater than to have the company of her who is the most dearly loved, knowing likewise that she by her choice holds the same, the thought of which greatly delights me.

Judge, therefore, what that very person shall do, whose absence hath so grieved my heart that neither tongue nor pen can express the hurt, which no other thing excepting that can ever cure. Praying you, my mistress, to say to my lord your father on my part that I beg of him to hasten by two days the time appointed, that he may be at Court before his former promise, or, at least, on the day already agreed. For otherwise I shall think he will not serve a lover's turn, as was his promise, nor will not allow of mine expectation.

No more at this present, for lack of time, trusting soon to tell you by word of mouth the residue of sufferings that I by your absence have sustained. Written with the hand of that secretary who wishes himself at this time private with you, and who is and always will be,

Your loyal and most assured servant,
H. autre (A B) ne cherche R.

8.

Darling, these shall be only to advertise you that this bearer and his fellow be dispatched with as many things to compass our matter, and to bring it to pass as our wits could imagine or devise; which brought to pass, as I trust, by their diligence, it shall be shortly, you and I shall have our desired end, which should be more to my heart's ease, and more quietness to my mind, than any other thing in this world; as, with God's grace, shortly I trust shall be proved, but not so soon as I would it were; yet I will ensure you there shall be no time lost that may be won, and further can not be done; for *ultra posse non est esse.* Keep him not too long with you, but desire him, for your sake, to make the more speed; for the sooner we shall have word from him, the sooner shall our matter come to pass. And thus upon trust of your short repair to London, I make an end of my letter, mine own sweet heart.

Written with the hand of him which desireth as much to be yours as you do to have him.

H.R.

9.

The unquietness I had from doubt of your good health troubled and distressed me not a little, and I should have had no rest had I not been ascertained thereof, but since as yet you have felt nothing I trust and am indeed well assured that it will cease where you are, as I trust it is doing here; for when we were at Waltham two ushers, two grooms-of-the-chamber, your brother and Master Treasurer sickened, and are now wholly restored; and since then we have returned to our house at Hunsdon, where we are right well bestowed without a single sick person at this hour, God be praised; and I believe that if you would retire from the parts of Surrey as we did you will pass it without danger. And there is also another thing that may comfort you, for in truth, as they say, few women or none have this malady, and, what is more, none of our Court and but few elsewhere have died thereof. Wherefore I implore you, my entirely beloved, to have no fear at all, nor to let our absence too much vex you, for wheresoever I may be I am yours; and notwithstanding one must sometimes submit to such ill-fortune, for whoso will struggle against fate at such a point is full often the further off from his desire, nevertheless comfort yourself and take courage, and banish this distemper so far as you can, and then I trust full soon to make us exult in its dismissal. No more at this present, for lack of time, but that I wish you in my arms, that I might a little relieve your inutile and vain thoughts.

Written with the hand of him who is and always will be your

Im HR mutable.

10.

News has come to me suddenly to-night, the most displeasant that could be brought, for the which of three reasons, I must needs lament. The first, to hear of the illness of my mistress, whom I do esteem more than all the world, whose health I desire as much as mine own, and the half of whose malady I would willingly bear to have you healed thereof. The second, for the fear I have to be yet again longer oppressed by absence, mine enemy, which to this present hath done me all possible annoy, and in so far as I can judge is determined to do worse, though I pray God to rid me of such an importunate rebel. The third, because the physician in whom I put most trust is now at this time absent when he could most do me pleasure, for by him and his assistance I should hope to obtain one of my chief joys in this world, which is, to have my mistress healed. Nevertheless, for lack of him, I send you the second, who alone remains, praying God that he may soon restore your health, and I shall accordingly hold him even more closely in my affection. Beseech-ing you to be governed by his advices in all things concerning your malady, by which doing I trust soon to see you again, which to me will be more sovereign remedy than all the precious stones in the world.

Written by that secretary who is and always will be

Your loyal and most assured servant,

H (AB) R.

11.

The cause of my writing at this time, good sweetheart, is only to understand of your good health and prosperity; whereof to know I would be as glad as in manner mine own, praying God (that and it be his pleasure) to send us shortly together, for I promise you I long for it. How be it, trust it shall not be long to; and seeing my darling is absent, I can no less do than to send her some flesh, representing my name, which is hart flesh for Henry, prognosticating that hereafter, God willing, you must enjoy some of mine, which, he pleased, I would I were now.

As touching your sister's matter, I have caused Walter Welche to write to my lord mine mind therein, whereby I trust that Eve shall not have power to deceive Adam; for surely, whatsoever is said, it cannot so stand, with his honour but that he must needs take her, his natural daughter, now in her extreme necessity.

No more to you at this time, mine own darling, but that with a wish I would we were together an evening.

With the hand of yours,
H.R.

12.

Since your last letters, mine own darling, Walter Welche, Master Brown, John Carey, Yrion of Brearton, and John Cocke, the apothecary, be fallen of the sweat in this house, and thanked be God, all well recovered, so that as yet the plague is not fully ceased here, but I trust shortly it shall. By the mercy of God, the rest of us yet be well, and I trust shall pass it, either not to have it, or at the least, as easily as the rest have done.

15. *Court dress of the Tudor period from Holbein's sketch-book.*

As touching the matter of Wilton, my lord Cardinal hath had the nuns before him and examined them, Mr Bell being present; which hath certified me that, for a truth, that she had confessed herself (which we would have had abbess) to have had two children by two sundry priests; and further, since hath been kept by a servant of the Lord Broke that was, and that not long ago. Wherefore I would not, for all the gold in the world, clog your con-science nor mine to make her ruler of a house, which is of so ungoodly demeanour; nor, I trust, you would not that neither for brother nor sister I should so distain mine honour or conscience. And as touching the prioress, or Dame Eleanor's eldest sister, though there is not any evident case proved against them, and that the prioress is so old that of many years she could not be as she was named; yet notwithstanding, to do you pleasure, I have done that neither of them shall have it, but that some other good and well-disposed woman shall have it, whereby the house shall be the better reformed (whereof I ensure you it had much need), and God much the better served.

As touching your abode at Hever, do therein as best shall like you, for you know best what air doth best with you; but I would it were come thereto (if it pleased God), that neither of us need care for that, for I ensure you I think it long. Suche is fallen sick of the sweat, and therefore I send you this bearer, because I think you long to hear tidings from us, as we do in likewise from you.

> Written with the hand de votre seul,
> H.R.

13.

Darling, I heartily recommend mè to you, ascertaining you that I am not a little perplexed with such things as your brother shall on my part declare unto you, to whom I pray you give full credence, for it were too long to write. In my last letters I writ to you that I trusted shortly to see you, which is better known at London than with any that is about me, whereof I not a little marvel; but lack of discreet handling must needs be the cause thereof. No more to you at this time, but that I trust shortly our meetings shall not depend upon other men's light handlings, but upon your own.

> Written with the hand of him that longeth to be yours,
> H.R.

14.

Mine own sweetheart, this shall be to advertise you of the great elengeness [loneliness] that I find here since your departing; for I ensure you methinketh the time longer since your departing now last than I was wont to do a whole fortnight. I think your kindness and my fervency of love causeth it; for other-wise I would not have thought it possible that for so little a while it should have grieved me. But now that I am coming towards you, methinketh my pains be half released, and also I am right well comforted in so much that my book maketh substantially for my matter; in looking whereof I have spent above four hours this day, which caused me now to write the shorter letter to you at this time, because of some pain in my head; wishing myself (specially an evening) in my sweetheart's arms, whose pretty dukkys [breasts] I trust shortly to cusse [kiss].

   Written with the hand of him that was, is, and shall be yours by his will,
                                                        H.R.

15.

Darling,
Though I have scant leisure, yet, remembering my promise, I thought it convenient to certify you briefly in what case our affairs stand. As touching a lodging for you, we have gotten one by my lord cardinal's means, the like whereof could not have been found hereabouts for all causes, as this bearer shall more show you. As touching our other affairs, I ensure you there can

16. *Another early portrait, by an unknown artist, now in the Musée Condé, of Anne Boleyn: the inspiration of the famous series of love letters which leave no doubt of the intensity of Henry's passion.*

be no more done, nor more diligence used, nor all manners of dangers better both foreseen and provided for, so that I trust it shall be hereafter to both our comforts, the specialities whereof were both too long to be written, and hardly by messenger to be declared. Wherefore, till your repair hither, I keep something in store, trusting it shall not be long to; for I have caused my lord, your father, to make his provisions with speed; and thus, for lack of time, darling, I make an end of my letter, written with the hand of him which I would were yours.

H.R.

16.

The reasonable request of your last letter, with the pleasure also that I take to know them true, causeth me to send you now these news. The legate which we most desire arrived at Paris on Sunday or Monday last past, so that I trust by the next Monday to hear of his arrival at Calais; and then I trust within a while after to enjoy that which I have so longed for, to God's pleasure, and both our comforts.

No more to you at this present, mine own darling, for lack of time, but that I would you were in mine arms, or I in yours, for I think it long since I kissed you.

17. *An elaborate design for a chimney-piece in Bridewell Palace: sometimes ascribed to Holbein.*

Written after the killing of an hart, at eleven of the clock, (minding, with God's grace, to-morrow, mightily timely to kill another) by the hand which I trust shortly shall be yours.

Henry R.

17.

To inform you what joy it is to me to understand of your conformableness to reason, and of the suppressing of your inutile and vain thoughts and fantasies with the bridle of reason. Wherefore, good sweetheart, continue the same, not only in this, but in all your doings hereafter; for thereby shall come, both to you and me, the greatest quietness that may be in this world.

The cause why this bearer tarrieth so long is the business that I have had to dress up gear for you; which I trust, ere long, to cause you occupy; and then I trust to occupy yours; which shall be recompense enough to me for all my pains and labours.

The unfeigned sickness of this well-willing legate doth somewhat retard his access to your presence; but I trust verily, when God shall send him health, he will with diligence recompense his demur. For I know well where he hath said (lamenting the saying and bruit that he should be imperial) that it should be well known in this matter that he is not imperial. And thus, for lack of time, sweetheart farewell. Written with the hand which fain would be yours, and so is the heart.

H.R.

Hall's *Chronicle*

Edward Hall was born towards the end of the fifteenth century and died in 1547, the same year as his king. He recorded the events of the reign faithfully, if uncritically, in his Chronicle of England. *These extracts are from the most important section of that Chronicle,* which Hall entitled The Triumphant Reign of Henry VIII.

THE TWENTY-EIGHTH YEAR, 1536-7

On May day were solemn jousts kept at Greenwich, and suddenly from the jousts the king departed having not above six persons with him, and came in the evening from Greenwich to his palace at Westminster. Of this sudden departing many men mused, but most chiefly the queen, who the next day was apprehended and brought from Greenwich to the Tower of London, where after she was arraigned of high treason, and condemned. Also at the same time was likewise apprehended, the Lord Rocheforde brother of the said queen, and Henry Norris, Mark Smeton, Wyllyam a Brutton and Sir

19. *A large painting of Henry VIII and his family in the style of Holbein. The picture was not painted from life, since Jane Seymour in fact died in childbirth. Henry, Jane and Edward are at the centre, and the two Princesses by earlier marriages are tactfully placed at either side.*

Francis Weston, all of the king's privy chamber. All these were likewise committed to the Tower and after arraigned and condemned of high treason. And all the gentlemen were beheaded on the scaffold at the Tower Hill: but the queen was with a sword beheaded within the Tower. And these following were the words that she spoke the day of her death which was the nineteenth day of May, 1536.

'Good Christian people, I am come hither to die, for according to the law, and by the law I am judged to die, and therefore I will speak nothing against it. I am come hither to accuse no man, nor to speak anything of that, whereof I am accused and condemned to die, but I pray God save the king and send him long to reign over you, for a gentler nor a more merciful prince was there never: and to me he was ever a good, a gentle and sovereign lord. And if any person will meddle of my cause, I require them to judge the best. And thus I take my leave of the world and of you all, and I heartedly desire you all to pray for me. O Lord have mercy on me, to God I commend my soul.' And then she knelt down saying: 'To Christ I commend my soul, Jesu receive my soul' divers times, till that her head was striken off with the sword. And on the Ascension day following, the king wore white for mourning.

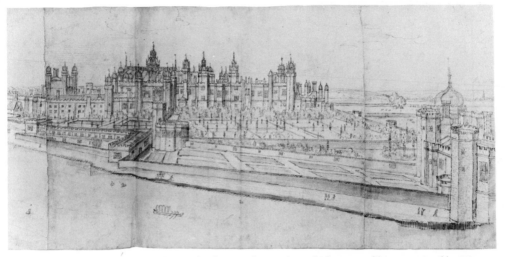

20. *Hampton Court by Wyngaerde: Wolsey's magnificent palace which was swiftly appropriated by Henry after the Cardinal's death.*

The week before Whitsuntide the king married Lady Jane daughter to the right worshipful Sir John Seymour knight, which at Whitsuntide was openly showed as queen.

The eighth day of June the king held his high Court of Parliament in the which parliament the king's two first marriages, that is to say with the Lady Catherine and with the Lady Anne Boleyn, were both judged unlawful, as more at large appeareth in the act in the book of statutes.

THE TWENTY-NINTH YEAR, 1537–8

In October on St Edward's evening was born at Hampton court the noble infant Prince Edward, whose godfathers at the christening were the Arch-bishop of Canterbury, and the Duke of Norfolk and his godmother the Lady Mary the king's daughter, and at the bishoping was godfather the Duke of Suffolk. At the birth of this noble prince was great fires made through the whole realm and great joy made with thanksgiving to Almighty God, which had sent so noble a prince to succeed to the crown of this realm: but Lord what lamentation shortly after was made for the death of his noble and gracious mother Queen Jane, which departed out of this life the fourteenth day of October, next following and of none in the realm was it more heavily taken than of the king's majesty himself, whose death caused the king im-mediately to remove unto Westminster, where he mourned and kept himself close and secret a great while: and the eighth day of November the corpse of the queen was carried to Windsor with great solemnity, and there was buried in the midst of the choir in the Castle Church: and at the same time was made . . . a solemn hearse for her, where was Mass and dirge, and in like manner was sung Mass and dirge in every parish church in London.

The king's majesty kept his Christmas at Greenwich in his mourning apparel, and so was all the Court till the morrow after Candlemas day, and then he and all other changed.

Also this year the Viscount Beauchamp was created Earl of Hertford and Sir William Fitzwilliam, High Admiral, created Earl of Southampton.

This year James, King of Scots, married the Lady Magdalene the French king's eldest daughter.

THE THIRTY-FIRST YEAR, 1539-40

The eleventh day of December at the turnpike on this side of Gravelines was the Lady Anne of Cleves received by the Lord Lysle, Deputy of the town of Calais, and with the spears and horsemen belonging to the retinue there, all being fresh and warlike apparelled, and so marching toward Calais a mile and more from the town met her grace the Earl of Southampton, Great Admiral of England, and apparelled in a coat of purple velvet cut on cloth of gold and tied with great aiglettes and trefoils of gold, to number of four hundred and baudrickwise he wore a chain, at the which did hang a whistle of gold set with rich stones of a great value. And in his company thirty gentlemen of the king's household very richly apparelled with great and massive chains, and in especially Sir Francis Bryan and Sir Thomas Seymour's chains were of great value and strange fashion. Besides this, the Lord Admiral had a great number of gentlemen in blue velvet and crimson

21. *Jane Seymour, Henry's third wife, who died shortly after giving birth to his only son, Edward.*

22. *Jane Seymour's drinking cup: a beautifully intricate design by Holbein which demonstrates his outstanding versatility.*

satin and his yeomen in damask of the same colours, and the mariners of his ship in satin of Bridges, both coats and slops of the same colours, which Lord Admiral with low obeisance welcomed her, and so brought her into Calais by the lantern gate, where the ships lay in the haven garnished with their banners, pensiles and flags, pleasantly to behold. And at her entry was shot such a peal of guns, that all the retinue much marvelled at it. And at her entry into the town, the Mayor of the town presented her with a hundred marks in gold. And before the staple hall stood merchants of the staple well apparelled, which likewise presented her with an hundred sovereigns of gold in a rich purse, which heartily thanked them, and so she rode to the king's place called the Checker, and there she lay fifteen days for lack of prosperous wind. During which time goodly jousts and costly banquets were made to her for her solace and recreation. And on St John's day in Christmas, she with one sail took passage about noon and landed at Deal in the downs about five of the clock, where Sir Thomas Cheyney, Lord Warden of the ports, received her, and there she tarried a space in a castle newly built, and thither came the Duke and Duchess of Suffolk and the Bishop of Chichester, with a great number of knights and esquires and ladies of Kent and others which welcomed her grace, and so that night brought her to Dover Castle, where she rested till Monday: on which day for all the storm that then was she marched toward Canterbury, and on Barain Down met her the Archbishop of Canterbury accompanied with the Bishop of Ely, St Asse, St Davies and Dover, and a great company of gentlemen well apparelled, and so brought her to St Austens without Canterbury, where she lay that night: and on the next day she came to Sittingbourne and there lodged the night. And as she passed toward Rochester on New Year's Eve, on Reynam Down met her the Duke of Norfolk and the Lord Dacre of the South, and the Lord Mountjoy with a great company of knights and squires of Norfolk and Suffolk, and the Barons of the Exchequer, all in coats of velvet with chains of gold, which brought her to Rochester where she lay in the palace all New Year's Day. On which day the king, which sore desired to see her grace, accompanied with no more than eight persons of his privy chamber, and both he and they all apparelled in marble coats privily came to Rochester, and suddenly came to her presence, which therewith was somewhat astonished: but after he had spoken and welcomed her, she with most gracious and loving countenance and behaviour him received and welcomed on her knees, whom he gently took up and kissed: and all that after noon communed and devised with her, and that night supped with her, and the next day he departed to Greenwich, and she came to Dartford.

On the morrow being the third day of January, and Saturday, in a fair plain on Black Heath more nearer the foot of Shooters Hill than the ascendent of the hill called Black Heath Hill, was pitched a rich cloth of gold and divers other tents and pavilions in the which were made fires and perfumes for her and such ladies as should receive her grace: and from the tents to the park gate of Greenwich were all bushes and firs cut down, and a large and ample way made for the show of all persons. And first next to the park pale on the East side, stood the merchants of the Stilyard: and on the West side stood the merchants of Jean, Florence and Venice, and the Spaniards, in coats of velvet. Then on both sides of the way stood the merchants of the City of London and aldermen with the counsellors of the said city to the number of an hundred and sixty which were mixed with the squires: next upward to-ward the tents stood knights: then the fifty gentlemen pensioners, and all this sort were apparelled in velvet and chains of gold, truly accounted to the number of twelve hundred and above, beside them that came with the king and her grace, which were six hundred in velvet coats and chains of gold. Behind the gentlemen stood the serving men in good order, well horsed and apparelled, that whosoever had well viewed them might say that they for tall and comely personages and clean of limb and body, were able to give the greatest prince in Christendom a mortal breakfast if he were the king's enemy: and of this sort the gentlemen appertaining to the Lord Chancellor,

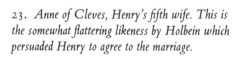
23. *Anne of Cleves, Henry's fifth wife. This is the somewhat flattering likeness by Holbein which persuaded Henry to agree to the marriage.*

the Lord Privy Seal and the Lord Admiral and divers other lords, beside the costly liveries and comely horses, wore chains of gold.

Thus was the lane ordered in ranks from the park gate toward the cross on the heath, which was between the ranks and the tents, and in this order they continued till the king and she were returned.

About twelve of the clock her grace with all the company which were of her own nation to the number of an hundred horse, and accompanied with the Dukes of Norfolk and Suffolk, the Archbishop of Canterbury and other bishops, lords and knights which had received and conveyed her as you have heard before, came down Shooters Hill toward the tents, and a good space from the tents met her the Earl of Rutland, her Lord Chamberlain, Sir Thomas Denyce, her Chancellor, and all her counsellors and officers, amongst whom, Doctor Daye appointed to her Almoner, made to her an eloquent oration in latin, and presenting to her on the king's behalf all the officers and servants: which oration was answered unto by the duke her brother's secretary there being present, which done, the Lady Margaret Douglas, daughter to the Queen of Scots, the Lady Marquis Dorset, daughter to the French queen being nieces to the king, and the Duchess of Richmond, and the Countess of Rutland and Hertford with divers other ladies and gentlewomen, to the number of sixtyfive saluted and welcomed her grace, which alighted out of her chariot in the which she had ridden all her long journey, and with most goodly demeanour and loving countenance gave to them hearty thanks and kissed them all, and after all her counsellors and officers kissed her hand, which done, she with all the ladies entered the tents, and there warmed them a space.

When the king knew that she was arrived in her tent, he with all diligence set out through the park. And first issued the king's trumpeters, then the king's officers being sworn of his counsel, next after them followed the

24. *Henry VIII's astrolabe carrying his coat of arms in the centre.*

gentlemen of the king's privy chamber, some apparelled in coats of velvet embroidered: others had their coats guarded with chains of gold, very rich to behold, which were well horsed and trapped: after them ensued barons, the youngest first, and so Sir William Hollys, knight, Lord Mayor of London, rode with the Lord Parr being youngest baron. Then followed bishops apparelled in black satin. Then immediately followed the earls, and then Duke Philippe of Bavyer and Count Palantyne of the Rhine, richly apparelled with the livery of the Toysant or Golden Fleece about his neck. Then followed the ambassadors of the French king and the emperor, next followed the Lord Privy Seal, Lord Cromwell, and the Lord Chancellor: then Garter King of Arms, and the other officers of arms and the sergeants at arms gave their attendance on every side of the lords: which lords for the most part were apparelled in purple velvet, the Lord Marquis Dorset in the same suite bore the king's sword of estate. After him a good distance followed the king's highness mounted on a goodly courser, trapped in rich cloth of gold traversed lattice wise square, all over embroidered with flat gold of damask, pearled on every side of the embroidery, the buckles and pendants were all of fine gold. His person was apparelled in a coat of purple velvet, somewhat made like a frock, all over embroidered with flat gold of damask with small lace mixed between of the same gold and other laces of the same so going traverse wise, that the ground little appeared: about which garment was a rich guard very curiously embroidered, the sleeves and breast were cut, lined with cloth of gold and tied together with great buttons of diamonds, rubies and orient pearl, his sword and swordgirdle adorned with stones and especial emeralds, his night cap garnished with stone, but his bonnet was so rich of jewels that few men could value them. Beside all this he wore in baudrikewise a collar of such ballasts and pearl that few men ever saw the like: and about his person ran ten footmen all richly apparelled in goldsmiths' work. And notwithstanding that this rich apparel and precious jewels were pleasant to the nobles and all other being present to behold, yet his princely countenance, his goodly personage and royal gesture so far exceeded all other creatures being present, that in comparison of his person, all his rich apparel was little esteemed. After him followed his Lord Chamberlain, then came Sir Anthony Browne, master of his horse, a goodly gentleman and a comely personage, well horsed, trapped and richly apparelled leading the king's horse of estate by a long reign of gold, which horse was, trapped in manner like a bard with crimson velvet and satin, all over embroidered with

gold after an antique fashion, very curiously wrought. Then followed the
pages of honour in coats of rich tinsel and crimson velvet paled, riding on
great coursers, all trapped in crimson velvet, embroidered with new devices
and knots of gold which were both pleasant and costly to behold. Then
followed Sir Anthony Wingfeld, Captain of the Guard, and then the
Guard well horsed and in rich coats. In this order the king rode to the last
end of the rank where the spears or pensioners stood: and there every person
that came with the king placed himself on the one side or the other, the king
standing in the midst.

When her grace was advertised of the king's coming, she issued out of her
tent being apparelled in a rich gown of cloth of gold, raised made round
without any train after the Dutch fashion, and on her head a kall and over
that a round bonnet or cap set full of Orient pearl of a very proper fashion,
and before that she had a coronet of black velvet, and about her neck she
had a portelet set full rich stone which glistened all the field. And at the door
of the tent, she mounted on a fair horse richly trapped, with her footmen
about her in goldsmiths' work embroidered with the black lion, and on his
shoulder a carbuncle gold, and so she marched toward the king: which
perceiving her to approach came forward somewhat beyond the cross on
Black Heath, and there paused a little in a fair place till she came nearer:
then he put off his bonnet and came forward to her, and with most lovely
countenance and princely behaviour saluted, welcomed and embraced her
to the great rejoicing of the beholders: and she likewise not forgetting her
duty, with most amiable aspect and womanly behaviour received his grace
with many sweet words and great thanks and praisings given to him. And
while they two were thus communing, the fifty pensioners and the Guard
departed to furnish the court and hall of Greenwich. And when the king
had talked with her a little while, he put her on his right hand, and so with
their footmen they rode as though they had been coupled together. O what
a sight was this to see so goodly a prince and so noble a king to ride with so
fair a lady of so goodly a stature and so womanly a countenance, and in
especial of so good qualities, I think no creature could see them but his heart
rejoiced.

Now when the king and she were met and both their companies joined
together, they returned through the ranks of knights and squires which
stood still all this while and removed not, in this order: first her trumpeters
went forward, which were twelve in number beside two kettle drums on

horseback, then followed the king's trumpeters, then the king's counsellors, then the gentlemen of the Privy Chamber, then the gentlemen of her grace's country in coats of velvet, all on great horses: after them the Mayor of London in crimson velvet with a rich collar, coupled with the youngest baron, then all the barons, next following bishops, then earls, with whom rode the Earls of Overstein and Waldocke, of her country, then dukes and the Archbishop of Canterbury and Duke Phillip of Bavire, next followed the ambassadors, then the Lord Marquis with the king's sword, next followed the king himself equally riding with his fair lady, and behind him rode Sir Anthony Browne with the king's horse of estate as you heard before, and behind her rode Sir John Dudley, Master of her Horse, leading her spare palfrey trapped in rich tissue down to the ground: after them followed the henchmen or pages of honour, then followed the Lady Margaret Douglas, the Lady Marquis Dorset, the Duchess of Richmond and Suffolk, the Countess of Rutland and Hertford, and other countesses; then followed her grace's chariot in the which she rode all her journey, well carved and gilt with arms of her country curiously wrought and covered with cloth of gold, all the horses were trapped with black velvet, and on them rode pages of honour in coats of velvet, in the which chariot rode two ancient ladies of her country: next after the chariot followed six ladies and gentlewomen of her country all richly apparelled with caps set with pearl, and great chains of divers fashions after the usage of their country, which were very fair of face, and with them rode six ladies of England well beseen. Then followed another chariot likewise gilt and furnished as the other was: after that chariot followed ten English ladies well apparelled, next them another chariot all covered with black cloth, and in that four gentlewomen which were her grace's chamberers:

25. *Holbein in his less familiar role as designer of jewellery: the design for a pendant incorporating an intricate monogram.*

26. *A miniature thought to be Catherine Howard: the fourth of Henry's wives, and the second to be executed for supposed infidelity.*

then followed all the remnant of the ladies, gentlewomen and maidens in a great number which did wear that day French whodes: last of all came another chariot all black with three launders appertaining to her grace: next after followed a horselitter of cloth of gold and crimson velvet upon velvet paled, with horses trapped accordingly which the king sent her. Then followed the serving men of her train, all clothed in black and on great horses.

In this order they rode through the ranks, and so through the park and at the late Freers wall all men alighted saving the king the two Masters of the Horse and the henchmen which rode to the hall's door, and the ladies rode to the court gate. And as they passed they beheld on the wharf how the citizens of London were rowing up and down on the Thames even before them, every craft in his barge garnished with banners, flags, streamers, pensiles and targets, some painted and beaten with the king's arms, some with her grace's arms, and some with the arms of their craft or Mystery. Beside the barges of every craft, there was a barge made like a ship, called the Bachelors barke, decked with cloth of gold, pennons, pensiles and targets in great number, on whom waited a foyst that shot great pieces of artillery. And in every barge was diverse sorts of instruments and children and men singing, which sang and played altogether as the king and the lady passed on the wharf, which sight and noise they much praised and allowed.

When the king and she were within the utter court, they alighted from their horses, and the king lovingly embraced her and kissed her, bidding her welcome to her own, and led her by her left arm through the hall which was furnished beneath the hearth with the king's Guard, and above the hearth with the fifty pensioners with their battle axes, and so brought her up to her privy chamber, where he left her for that time.

And as soon as the king and she was entered the court, was shot out of the Tower of Greenwich and there about, a great peal of guns.

When the king's company and hers was entered the park, as you have heard, then all the horse men on Black Heath brake their array and had licence to depart to London, or to their lodging. To see how long it was or the horsemen could pass, and how late it was in the night the footmen could get over London Bridge, I assure you it was wondrous to behold, the number was so great.

This the noble lady remained unmarried until the Tuesday following being the day of the Epiphany: on which day about eight of the clock in the morning, his grace being apparelled in a gown of cloth of gold, raised with great flowers of silver, furred with black Jeneltis his coat crimson satin all to cut and embroidered and tied with great diamonds, and a rich collar about his neck, came solemnly with his nobility into the gallery next the closets, and there paused.

Then the lords went to fetch the Lady Anne, which was apparelled in a gown of rich cloth of gold set full of large flowers of great and Orient pearl, made after the Dutch fashion round, her hair hanging down, which was fair, yellow and long: on her head a coronal of gold replenished with great stone, and set about full of branches of rosemary, about her neck and middle, jewels of great value and estimation. In this apparel she going between the Earl of Overstein and the Grand Master Hostonden, which had the conduct and order of the performance of her marriage, with most demure countenance and sad behaviour, passed through the king's chamber, all the lords going before her till they came to the gallery where the king was, to whom she made three low obeisances and curtsies. Then the Archbishop of Canterbury received them and married them together, and the Earl of Overstein did give her: and about her marrying the king was written: God send me well to keep.

When the marriage was celebrated, they went hand in hand into the king's closet and there heard Mass and offered their tapers, and after Mass had wine and spices, and that done, the king departed to his chamber, and all the ladies waited on her to her chamber, the Duke of Norfolk going on the right hand, and the Duke of Suffolk on the left hand of her grace.

After nine of the clock, the king with a gown of rich tissue lined with crimson velvet embroidered, came to his closet, and she in her here in the same apparel that she was married in, came to her closet with her Sergeant-of-Arms and all her officers, like a queen, before her. And so the king and she went openly on procession and offered and dined together. And after dinner she changed into a gown like a man's gown, of tissue with long sleeves girt to her, furred with rich sables, her narrow sleeves were very costly, but on her head she had a cap as she wore on the Saturday before with a coronet of lawn, which cap was so rich of pearl and stone that it was judged to be of great value. And after her fashion, her ladies and gentlewomen were apparelled very rich and costly with chains of divers fashions, and in this apparel she went that night to Evensong, and after supped with the king: and after supper were Bankettes masks, and diverse disports, till the time came that it pleased the king and her to take their rest.

Henry to Katherine Parr, 1544

In July 1544 Henry joined his troops in their campaign against France. He wrote few personal letters in the later years of his life; this one, to the last of his six wives, gives a good picture of a king very much in control of events, militarily and diplomatically.

Most dearly and most entirely beloved wife, we recommend us heartily unto you, and thank you as well for your letter written unto us by your servant Robert Warner as for the venison which you sent then by him, and now last by Fowler, servant unto our dearest son the prince, for the which we give unto you our hearty thanks, and would have written unto you again a letter with our own hand, but that we be so occupied, and have so much to do in foreseeing and caring for everything ourself, as we have almost no manner rest or leisure to do any other thing.

The cause why we have detained here so long your said servant hath been upon hope to have sent you by him good news of the taking of the town, which no doubt we should have done, by the grace of God, before this time, but that our provision of powder is not come out of Flanders as we thought it would. Within two or three days we look for it here, and then shortly after we trust to write unto you some good news. And yet, in the mean season, we have done somewhat of importance, for we have won (and that without any loss of men) the strongest part of the town, which is the bray [outwork] of the castle – such a piece, and of such strength, as now that we have it in our hands we think four hundred of our men within it shall be able to keep it against four thousand of our enemies, and yet it is much weaker to the castle side than it was outward to us.

onfitebor tibi in feculum quia fecisti
& expectabo nomen tuum quoniam bonu est
in confpectu fanctorum tuorum Gloria
patti Sicut erat.

Di
xit
infipies
in corde
suo nō
est Deꝰ
Cor-
ruptisūt

27. An illumination from
Henry's psalter, now in the
British Museum, showing Henry
in old age, depicted with his jester,
Will Summers.

KATHARINE PARRE

Katherine Parr. A handsome
trait of Henry's last wife.

It lieth afore the castle, which hath no loop or flank to beat it, so as our men be in it in safety in some part thereof, but not in all, having the dyke at our commandment but not with sure biding in it, both for the top of the castle and a ring that goeth about it; for which ring there is good hoping, for we would fain have it, and they be loath to lose it: so sometime it is ours and another time theirs; but yet we trust to set them by it. But hitherto they have hardily defended it, and fought hand to hand for it, much manfuller than other Burgundian or Flemings would have done; for such as we have of them will do no good where any danger is, nor yet abide there with their will. This, and lying in another place within their first dyke, and almost as well entered the second, is hitherto as far forth as hath been done, saving that we lie so nigh them round about the town that we take more hurt with stones than ordnance.

Further, the French king is very desirous of a peace, and maketh much suit unto us for the same, insomuch as he hath sent unto us a letter of his own hand, desiring by the same a safe-conduct for certain notable personages to repair unto us from him in ambassade: that is to say, the Cardinal of Bellay, the premier president of Rouen, the premier treasurer of all the finances of France, the Captain of the Guard to the Dauphin, being a Gentleman of his Privy Chamber, and one of his principal secretaries, who be come hitherward on their way to Abbeville, attending for our safe-conduct, which

29. Henry's writing-desk, beautifully decorated in painted leather, now in the Victoria and Albert Museum.

we have sent to them, and have appointed our castle of Hardelow (whereof you have been advertised heretofore) for them to repair unto, and fifty horses in their company, twenty to be lodged within our said castle and the rest abroad in other places at our appointment.

And for because the said French king has promised to use our advice for the making of his appointment with the emperor, we have of late written to our ambassador with him to know what things he will demand, which he hath sent to us in certain articles touched somewhat with the extremist; and we again have, upon his desire to know our demand in case the French men would sue to him for peace, sent to him for our demands certain articles containing to have satisfaction of the arrangements due unto us for our pension, with all manner damages and interests which we have sustained by reason of the wars, and also the realm of France, with the duchies of Normandy, Aquitaine and Guienne, which demands we have made to meet with the extremity of the emperor's demands, which be so sore, as it should appear, that either he mindeth to have no peace, or that, if any peace should be treated, he would pluck the honour of the compounding of it out of our hand, notwithstanding that the matter was committed to us by the French king's suit, and that also, as the French king sayeth, he never made means to the emperor for a peace; all which these our advertisements we pray you communicate unto our Council attendant upon you there.

And whereas you desired to know our pleasure for the accepting into your chamber of certain ladies in places of others that cannot well give their attendance by reason of sickness; albeit we think those whom you have named unto us as unable almost to attend by reason of weakness as the others be, yet we remit the accepting of them to your own choice, thinking, nevertheless, that though they shall not be meet to serve, yet you may, if you think so good, take them into your chamber to pass the time sometime with you at play, or otherwise to accompany you for your recreation.

As touching your request made unto us for Archer's wife, we are content, at your desire, to stay the giving from her of those things you wrote for, and so may you do there until you hear further of our pleasure in case any person would sue to have any of them.

At the closing up of these our letters the castle aforenamed, with the dyke, is at our commandment, and not like to be recovered by the Frenchmen again, as we trust, not doubting with God's grace but that the castle and town shall shortly follow the same trade, for as this day, which is the eighth day of

September, we begin three batteries, and have three mines going, besides one which hath done his execution in shaking and tearing off one of their greatest bulwarks. No more to you at this time, sweetheart, both for lack of time and great occupation of business, saving we pray you to give in our name our hearty blessings to all our children, and recommendations to our cousin Margaret and the rest of the ladies and gentlewomen, and to our Council also.

Written with the hand of your loving husband,
HENRY R.

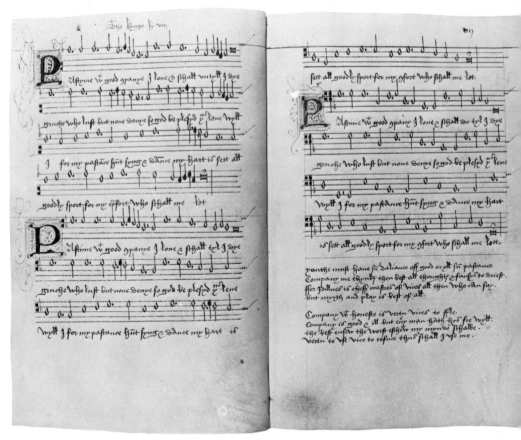

30. 'Pastance with good Company.' Both music and words seem to be Henry's own work.

Song: 'Pastance with good Company'

Henry VIII was an accomplished musician, and the following song sets out the somewhat hedonistic ideals of his youth.

Pastance with good company
I love and shall until I die
Grudge who will, but none deny,
So god be pleased this life will I
   For my pastance,
   Hunt, sing, and dance,
   My heart is set,
   All goodly sport
   To my comfort
   Who shall me let?

Youth will needs have dalliance,
Of good or ill some pastance;
Company me thinketh best
All thought and fancies to digest,
   For idleness
   Is chief mistress
   Of vices all;
   Then who can say
   But pass the day
   Is best of all?

Company with honesty
Is virtue – and vice to flee;
Company is good or ill
But every man hath his free will.
   The best I sue,
   The worst eschew;
   My mind shall be
   Virtue to use;
   Vice to refuse
   I shall use me.

EDWARD VI

Edward, born in 1537 to Henry VIII and Jane Seymour, inherited the throne at the age of nine and died just six years later. Physically he was never strong, and naturally enough was never in control of events, dominated as he was in turn by the Dukes of Somerset and Northumberland. But it would be wrong to dismiss him as without significance. Following the upheavals of his father's reign, the future of the Reformation was by no means certain. Under Edward the 'advanced' party of Reformers were able to progress to a new doctrinal radicalism which would have been impossible without Edward's own support. Young though he was, the fact remains he was a convinced Protestant. He was perfectly prepared to note, in his aloof way, the religious improvements undertaken and the constraints on the Catholic practice of his half-sister Mary. In effect, his reign helped to ensure that the break with Rome would be permanent and that Mary's attempt to reverse it would prove no more than an interlude.

Edward VI was unique among Tudor sovereigns in that he kept a diary or Chronicle which runs from when he was twelve and five months to about a month after his fifteenth birthday, just before the onset of his fatal illness. It is not an intimate document but an abrupt and summary record of events, probably started at the time of his coronation with the first paragraph added later. Its significance is, in the words of W. K. Jordan, 'not only in the subject matter itself and from its significance as a historical source, but because it is quite un-self-consciously the clear and moving record of the shaping and maturing of a precocious mind and temperament'. Only part of the last year (1552) is included here, the text taken from Professor W. K. Jordan's fine and fully annotated edition which should be consulted by anyone wishing to read the Chronicle in its entirety.

31. A Holbein portrait of Edward at the age of six, three years before his accession.

Edward's *Chronicle*

1. Orders was taken with the chandlers of London for selling there tallow candles, which before some denied to do; and some were punished with imprisonment.

3. The challenge that was made in the last month was fulfilled. The challengers were:

The Earl of Warwick	Sir Harry Neville
Sir Harry Sidney	Sir Harry Gates

Defendants

The Lord William [Howard]	Sir Will. Stafford
The Lord Fitzwalter	Sir John Perrot
The Lord Ambrose [Dudley]	Mr Norris
The Lord Robert [Dudley]	Mr Digby
The Lord FitzWarren	Mr Warcopp
Sir G[eorge] Howard	Mr Courtney

Mr Knollys
The Lord Braye
Mr Paston
Mr Carey
Sir Anthony Browne
Mr Drury

These, eighteen in all, ran six courses apiece at tilt against the challengers, and accomplished their courses right well, and so departed again.

5. There were sent to Guînes Sir Richard Cotton and Mr Braye to take view of Calais, Guînes, and the marches, and with advice of the captains and engineers to devise some amendment, and thereupon to make me certificate, and upon mine answer to go further [in]to the matter.

4. It was appointed that if Mr Stanhope lost Hull, then that I should no

32. *Edward Seymour, Duke of Somerset: the young King's first Protector until his downfall in 1549.*

33. *The coronation procession of Edward VI – a watercolour copy of a wall-painting once in Cowdray Hall, Sussex.*

more be charged therewith, but that the town should take it and should have £40 a year for the repairing of the castle.

2. I received letters out of Ireland, which appear in the Secretary's hand. And thereupon the Earldom of Thomond was by me given from O'Brien's heirs, whose father was dead, and had it for term of life, to Donough, Baron of Ibrachan, and his heirs male. Also letters were written of thanks to the Earls of Desmond and Clanricard and to the Baron of Dungannon.

3. The Emperor's ambassador moved me severally that my sister Mary might have mass, which, with no little reasoning with him, was denied him.

6. The foresaid challengers came in to the tourney, and the foresaid defendants entered in after[ward] with two more with them – Mr Tyrrell and Mr Robert Hopton – and fought right well, and so the challenge was accomplished. The same night was first a play; after a talk between one that was called Riches, and the other Youth, whether [one] of them was better. After some pretty reasoning there came in six champions of either side:

On Youth's side came:

My Lord Fitzwalter	Sir William Cobham
My Lord Ambrose [Dudley]	Mr Carey
Sir Anthony Browne	Warcopp

On Riches' side:

My Lord FitzWarren	Digby
Sir Robert Stafford	Hopton
Mr Courtney	Hungerford

All these fought two to two at barriers in the hall. Then came in two apparelled like Almains: the Earl of Ormonde and Jacques Granado; and two came in like friars; but the Almains would not suffer them to pass till they had fought. The friars were Mr Drury and Thomas Cobham. After this followed two masques: one of men, another of women. Then a banquet of 120 dishes. This was the end of Christmas.

7. I went to Deptford to dine there and break up the hall.

8. Upon a certain contention between Lord Willoughby and Sir Andrew Dudley, Captain of Guînes, for their jurisdiction, the Lord Willoughby was sent for to come over to the intent the controversy might cease and order might be taken.

12. There was a commission granted to the Earl of Bedford, and to the Mr Vice-Chamberlain, and certain other, to call in my debts that were owing me, and the days past, and also to call in those that be past when the days be come.

17. There was a match run between six gentlemen of a side at tilt.

Of one side	Of the other side
The Earl of Warwick	The Lord Ambrose
The Lord Robert [Dudley]	The Lord Fitzwalter
Mr Sidney	Sir Francis Knollys
Mr Neville	Sir Anthony Browne
Mr Gates	Sir John Perrot
Anthony Digby	Mr Courtney.
These won by 4 taints.	

18. The French ambassador moved that we should destroy the Scottish part of the Debatable Ground, as they had done ours. It was answered, first, the Lord Conyers, that made the agreement, made it none otherwise but as it should stand with his superior's pleasure. Whereupon, the same agreement being misliked because the Scottish part was much harder to overcome, word was sent to stay the matter; nevertheless the Lord Maxwell did upon malice to the English Debatables overrun them. Whereupon was concluded that, if the Scots will agree it, the ground shall be divided; if not, then shall the Scots waste their Debatables, and we ours, commanding them by proclamation to depart.

This day the Steelyard put in their answer to a certain complaint that the Merchant Adventurers laid against them.

19. The Bishop of Ely, *custos sigilli*, was made Chancellor because as *custos*

34. *A tilt match in progress: a contemporary view showing the way in which these tournaments were mounted.*

35. *A woodcut illustration, taken from an early history, which gives a brief and pithy summary of the reign of the Protestant boy king.*

sigilli he could execute nothing in the Parliament that should be done but only to seal ordinary things.

21. Removing to Westminster.

22. The Duke of Somerset had his head cut off upon Tower Hill between eight and nine o'clock in the morning.

16. Sir William Pickering delivered a token to the Lady Elizabeth – a fair diamond.

18. The Duke of Northumberland, having under him 100 men of arms and 100 light horse, gave up the keeping of fifty men-at-arms to his son, the Earl of Warwick.

23. The sessions of Parliament began.

24. John Gresham was sent over into Flanders to show to the Fuggers, to whom I owe money, that I would defer it or, if I paid it, pay it in English to make them keep up their French crowns, with which I minded to pay them.

25. The answer of the Steelyard was delivered to certain of my learned Council to look on and oversee.

27. Sir Ralph Vane was condemned of felony in treason, answering like a ruffian.

Paris arrived with horses and showed how the French king had sent me six curtals, two Turks, a Barbary, two jennets, a stirring horse, and two little mules, and showed them to me.

29. Sir Thomas Arundel was likewise cast of felony in treason, after long controversy; for the matter was brought in trial by seven of the clock in the morning [of the] 28th day; at noon the quest went together; they sat shut up together in a house, without meat or drink, because they could not agree, all that day and all night; this 29th day in the morning they did cast him.

FEBRUARY

2. There was a King-of-Arms made for Ireland, whose name was Ulster, and his province was all Ireland, and he was the first fourth King-of-Arms and the first Herald of Ireland.

The emperor took the last month and this a million of pounds in Flanders.
6. It was appointed that Sir Philip Hoby should go to the regent upon pretense of ordering of quarrels of merchants, bringing with him £63,000 in French crowns to be paid in Flanders at Antwerp to the Schetz and their family of debts I owe them, to the intent he might dispatch both under one.
8. Sir Miles Partridge was condemned of felony for the Duke of Somerset's matter, for he was one of the conspirators.
8. Fifty men-at-arms appointed to Mr Sadler.
9. John Beaumont, Master of the Rolls, was put in prison for forging a false deed from Charles Brandon, Duke of Suffolk, to the Lady Anne Powis of certain lands and leases.

36. *A political allegory, showing the Protestant, Edward VI confounding the Pope after Henry's death. Interesting for the likenesses of his Council including Seymour, Somerset, Archbishop Cranmer and Dudley.*

10. Commission was granted out to thirty-two persons to examine, correct, and set forth the ecclesiastical laws. The persons' names were these:

The Bishops	*The Divines*
Canterbury	Taylor of Lincoln
Ely	Taylor of Hadleigh
London	Mr Cox, almoner
Winchester	Sir John Cheke
Exeter	Sir Anthony Cooke
Bath	Petrus Martyr
Gloucester	Johannes à Lasco
Rochester	Parker of Cambridge

Civilians	*Lawyers*
Mr Secretary Petre	Justice Bromley
Mr Secretary Cecil	Justice Hales
Mr Traheron	Gosnold
Mr Reed	Goodrich
Mr Cook	Stamford
May, Dean of [St] Paul's	Caryll
Skinner	Lucas
	Gawdy

10. Sir Philip Hoby departed with somewhat more crowns than came to 53,500 and odd pounds and had authority to borrow in my name of Lazarus Tucker £10,000 Flemish at 7 in the 100, for six months, to make up the pay, and to employ that that was in bullion to bring over with him. Also, to carry 3,000 mark weight upon a license the emperor granted the Schetz, which they did give me. After that to depart to Bruges, where the regent lay, and there to declare to her the griefs [of] my subjects.

11. There was delivered of armour, by John Gresham, merchant, 1,100 pairs of corselets and horsemen harnesses, very fair.

14. It was appointed that the 'Jesus of Lübeck', a ship of 800 tons, and the 'Mary Gonston' of 600 tons, should be let out for one voyage to merchantmen for £1,000, they at the voyage to Levant end to answer the tackling [of] the ship, the ordnance, munition, and to leave it in that case they took it. Certain other of the worst of my ships were appointed to be sold.

9. Proclamation was made at Paris that the bands of the dauphin, the Duke

of Vendôme, the Count d'Enghien, the Constable of France, the Duke of Guise and of Aumale, the Count of Sancerre, the Maréchal St. André, Mons. de Jarnac's, and Tavannes', should, the 15th day of March, assemble at Troyes in Champagne to resist the emperor. Also that the French king would go thither in person with 200 gentlemen of his household and 400 archers of his guard.

16. The French king sent his secretary, de l'Aubespine, to declare this voyage to him [Mr Pickering], and to desire him to take pains to go with him and to be a witness of his doings.

19. Whereupon it was appointed that he should have 2,000 crowns for his furnishment besides his diet, and Barnaby 800.

20. The Countess of Pembroke died.

18. The Merchant Adventurers put in their replication to the Steelyard's answer.

23. A decree was made by the board that, upon knowledge and information of their charters, they had found: first, that they were no sufficient corporation. Secondarily, their number, names, and nation was unknown. Thirdly, that when they had forfeited their liberties King Edward the Fourth did restore them on this condition: [that they] should color no strangers' goods, which they had done. Also that, whereas in the beginning they shipped not past eight cloths, after 100, after 1,000, after that 6,000, now in their names were shipped 14,000 cloths in one year, and but 1,100 of all other strangers. For these considerations, sentence was given that they had forfeited their liberties and were in like case with other strangers.

28. There came ambassadors from Hamburg and Lübeck to speak on the behalf of the Steelyard merchants.

29. A Fleming would have searched the 'Falcon' for Frenchmen. The 'Falcon' turned, shot off, boarded the Fleming, and took him.

Payment was made of £63,500 Flemish to the Fuggers, all saving £6,000, which he borrowed in French crowns, by Sir Philip Hoby.

MARCH

2. The Lord of Abergavenny was committed to ward for striking the Earl of Oxford in the chamber of presence.

The answer for the ambassadors of the Steelyard was committed to the Lord Chancellor, the two Secretaries, Sir Robert Bowes, Sir John Baker, Judge Montagu, Griffith Solicitor, Gosnold, Goodrich, and Brooke.

3. It was agreed that for better dispatch of things certain of the Council, with others joined with them, should overlook the penal laws and put certain of them in execution. Other should answer suitors; other should oversee my revenues and the order of them, and also the superfluous, and the payments heretofore made; other should have commission for taking away superfluous bulwarks.

1. Order was given, for defense of the merchants, to send four barks and two pinnaces to the sea.

4. The Earl of Westmorland, the Lord Wharton, the Lord Conyers, Sir Thomas Palmer, and Sir Thomas Chaloner were appointed in commission to meet with the Scottish ambassadors for the equal division of the ground that was called the Debatable.

6. The French ambassador declared to the Duke of Northumberland how the French king had sent him a letter of credit for his ambassador. After delivery made of the letter, he declared how Duke Maurice of Saxony, the Duke of Mecklenburg, the Marquis of Brandenburg, the Count of Mansfeld, and divers other princes of Germany had made a league with his master, offensive and defensive: the French to go to Strassburg with 30,000 footmen and 8,000 horsemen, the Almains to meet with them there the 25th of this month, with 15,000 footmen and 5,000 horsemen. Also the city of Strassburg had promised them victuals; and [he] declared how the French king would send me ambassadors to have me into the same league. Also that the Marquis

37. *A graphic sketch by Holbein showing a merchant ship of the period.*

of Brandenburg and Count of Mansfeld had been privily conveyed to the French king's presence and were again departed to levy men, and he thought by this time they were in the field.

10. He declared the same thing to me in the same manner.

9. It was consulted touching the marts, and it was agreed that it was most necessary to have a mart in England for the enriching of the same, to make it the more famous, and to be less in other men's danger, and to make all things better cheap and more plentiful. The time was thought good to have it now, because of the wars between the French king and the emperor. The places [which] were thought meetest: Hull for the east parts, Southampton for the south parts of England, as appeareth by two bills in my study. London also was thought no ill place; but it was appointed to begin with the other two.

11. The bills put up to the parliament were overseen and certain of them were for this time thought meet to pass and to be read; other, for avoiding tediousness, to be omitted and no more bills to be taken.

15. Those that were appointed commissioners for the requests or for execu-tion of penal laws or for overseeing of the courts received their commissions at my hand.

18. It was appointed that for the payment of £14,000 in the end of April there should be made an anticipation of the subsidy of London and of the lords of my Council, which should go near to pay the same with good provision.

20. The French ambassador brought me a letter of credit from his master and thereupon delivered me the articles of the league betwixt the Germans

38. *A contemporary view of Calais, in Edward's day still an English foothold on the Continent.*

and him, desiring me to take part of the same league, which articles I have also in my study.

23. The merchants of England, having been long stayed, departed – in all about sixty sail, the wool fleet and all – to Antwerp. They were counter-manded because of the mart, but it was too late.

24. Forasmuch as the exchange was stayed by the emperor to Lyons, the merchants of Antwerp were sore afraid; and, that the mart could not be without exchange, liberty was given to the merchants to exchange and rechange money for money.

26. Harry Dudley was sent to the sea with four ships and two barques for defense of the merchants, which were daily before robbed, who, as soon as he came to the sea, took two pirates' ships and brought them to Dover.

28. I did deny after a sort the request to enter into war, as appeareth by the copy of my answer in the study.

29. To the intent the ambassador might more plainly understand my meaning, I sent Mr Hoby and Mr Mason to him to declare him my intent more amply.

31. The Commissioners for the Debatable of the Scottish side did deny to meet, except a certain castle or pile might be first razed; whereupon letters were sent to stay our Commissioners from the meeting till they had further word.

10. Duke Maurice mustered at Arnstadt in Saxony all his own men – and left Duke August, the Duke of Anhalt, and the Count of Mansfeld – for defense of his country, chiefly for fear of the Bohemians. The young Landgrave Reiffenberg and other mustered in Hesse.

14. The Marquis Albert of Brandenburg mustered his men two leagues from Erfurt and after entered the same, receiving of the citizens a gift of 20,000 florins, and he borrowed of them 60,000 florins, and so came to Schweinfurt, where Duke Maurice and all the German princes were assembled.

APRIL

2. I fell sick of the measles and the smallpox.

4. Duke Maurice with his army came to Augsburg, which town was at the first yielded to him and delivered into his hands, where he did change certain officers, restored their preachers, and made the town more free.

5. The Constable with the French army came to Metz, which was within

39. *A view after Wyngaerde showing the meadows and country s[...] surviving round Westminster Palace in the 1550s.*

two days yielded to him, where he found great provision of victuals, and that he determined to make the staple of victual for his journey.

8. He came to a fort wherein was an abbey called Gorze, and that fort abide[d] eighty cannon shot, at length came to a parley, where the Frenchmen got it, won it by assault, slew all save fifteen with the captain, whom he hung.

9. He took a fort called Marange and razed it.

12. The French king came to Nancy to go to the army and there found the Duchess and the young Duke of Lorraine.

13. The Maréchal St André, with 200 men of arms and 2,000 footmen, carried away the young duke, accompanied with few of his old men, toward France, to the dauphin which lay at Reims, to the no little discontentation of his mother, the duchess. He fortified also divers towns in Lorraine and put in French garrisons.

14. He departed from Nancy to the army, which lay at Metz.

7. Mons. Senarpont gave an overthrow to the captain of St Omer, having with him 600 footmen and 200 horsemen.

15. The parliament broke up, and because I was sick and not able to go well abroad as then, I signed a bill containing the names of the acts which I would have pass, which bill was read in the House.

16. Also I gave commission to the Lord Chancellor, two archbishops, two bishops, two dukes, two marquises, two earls, and two barons to dissolve wholly this parliament.

18. The Earl of Pembroke surrendered his mastership of the horse, which I bestowed on the Earl of Warwick.

19. Also he left fifty of his men of arms, of which twenty-five were given to Sir Philip Hoby and twenty-five to Sir John Gates.

21. It was agreed that commissions should go out for to take certificate of the superfluous church plate to my use and to see how it has been embezzled.

The French ambassador desired that, forasmuch as it was dangerous carrying of victuals from Boulogne to Ardres by land, that I would give license to carry by sea to Calais, and so from Calais to Ardres on my ground.

22. The Lord Paget was degraded from the Order of the Garter for divers his offenses, and chiefly because he was no gentleman of blood, neither of father's side nor mother's side.

Sir Anthony St Leger, who was accused by the Bishop of Dublin for divers brawling matters, was taken again into the Privy Chamber and sat amongst the Knights of the Order.

23. Answer was given to the French ambassador that I could not accomplish his desire, because it was against my league with the emperor.

24. The Order of the Garter was wholly altered, as appears by the new statutes. There were elected Sir Andrew Dudley and the Earl of Westmorland.

26. Mons. de Courrières came from the Regent [of the Netherlands] to desire that her fleet might safely upon occasion take harbour in my havens. Also he said he was come to give order for redressing all complaints of our merchants.

25. Whereas it was appointed that the £14,000 I owed in the last of April should be paid, by the anticipation of the subsidy of London and of the Lords, because to exchange the same oversea was [a] loss of the six[th] part of the money I did so send over, stay was made thereof and the payment appointed to be made out of £20,000 Flemish which I took up there, [at] 14 *per centum*, and so remained £6,000 thereof to be paid there the last of May.

30. Removing to Greenwich.

28. The charges of the mints were diminished £1,400, and there was left £600.

18. King Ferdinand, Maximilian his son, and the Duke of Bavaria came to Linz to treat with Duke Maurice for a peace, where Maurice declared his griefs.

16. Duke Maurice's men received an overthrow at Ulm, whereupon Marquis Albert spoiled the country and gave them a day to answer.

31. A debt of £14,000 was paid to the Fuggers.

40. *A fine State portrait of Edward as King, from the Royal Collection, attributed to Guilim Stretes.*

MAY

1. The Steelyard men received their answer, which was to confirm the former judgment of my Council.

2. A letter was sent to the Fuggers from my Council to this effect: that I had paid £63,000 Flemish in February and £14,000 in April, which came to £87,000 [*sic*] Flemish, which was a fair sum of money to be paid in one year, chiefly in this busy world, wheras [money] is most necessary to be had for princes; besides this, that it was thought money should not now do him so much pleasure as at another time peradventure. Upon these considerations they had advised me to pay but £5,000 of the 45,000 I now owe and so to put over the rest according to the old interest, 14 *per cent.*, with which they desired him to take patience.

4. Mons. de Courrières received his answer, which was that I had long ago given order that the Flemish ships should not be molested in my havens, as it appeared because Frenchmen chasing Flemings into my havens could not get them because of the rescue they had. But that I thought it not convenient to have more ships to come into my havens than I could well rule and govern. Also a note of divers complaints of my subjects was delivered to him.

10. Letters were sent to my ambassadors that they should move to the princes of Germany, to the emperor, and to the French king, that if this treaty came to any effect or end I might be comprehended in the same.

Commission was given to Sir John Gates, Sir Robert Bowes, the Chancellor of the Augmentation, Sir Walter Mildmay, [and] Sir Richard Cotton to sell some part of the chantry lands and of the houses for the payment of my debts, which was £251,000 sterling at the least.

Taylor, Dean of Lincoln, was made Bishop of Lincoln.

Hooper, Bishop of Gloucester, was made Bishop of Worcester and Gloucester.

Scory, Bishop of Rochester, was made Bishop of Chichester.

Sir Robert Bowes was appointed to be Master of the Rolls.

7. Commandment was given to the Treasurers that nothing of the subsidy should be disbursed but by warrant from [the] board, and likewise for Our Lady Day revenues.

14. The Baron of the Exchequer, upon the surrender made by Justice Lyster, made chief justice; the attorney, chief baron; the solicitor general, attorney; and the solicitor of the Augmentation Gosnold, general solicitor; and no more solicitors to be in the Augmentation Court. Also there were

appointed eight sergeants of the law against Michaelmas next coming: Gawdy, Stamford, Caryll.

16. The muster was made of all the men-at-arms, saving fifty of Mr Sadler's, twenty-five of Mr Vice-Chamberlain, and twenty-five [of] Sir Philip Hoby, and also of all the pensioners.

17. The progress was appointed to be by Portchester to Poole in Dorsetshire and so through Salisbury homeward to Windsor.

18. It was appointed that money should be cried down in Ireland after a pay which was of money at midsummer next; in the mean season the thing to be kept secret and close. Also that Pirry, the mint master, taking with him Mr Brabazon, Chief Treasurer of the realm, should go to the mines and see what profit may be taken of the ore that the Almains had dug in a mine of silver; and if it would quit cost or more, to go forward withal; if not, to leave off and discharge all the Almains.

Also that 500 of the 2,000 soldiers there being should be cut off, and as many more as would go serve the French king or the emperor, leaving sufficient at home. No fortifications to be made also yet for a time in no place unfortified; and many other articles were concluded for Ireland.

20. Sir Richard Wingfield, Rogers, and [Sir Andrew Dudley] were appointed to view the state of Portsmouth, and to bring again their opinions touching the fortifying thereof.

4. The French king, having passed the straits of Lorraine, came to Saverne,

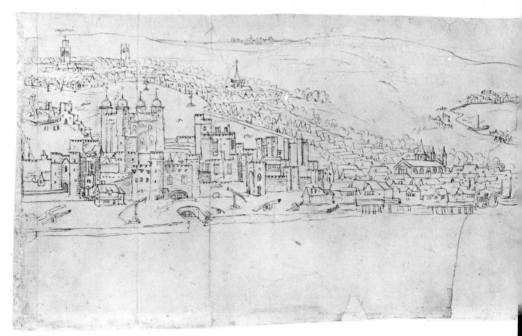

41. *A section of a panorama of London by Antony van den Wyngaerde, showing the Tower of London and Traitor's Gate in detail as well as a general view of the City.*

four miles from Strassburg and was victualed by the country but denied of passage through their town.

21. Answer came from the Fuggers that for the deferring of £30,000, parcel of 45,000, he was content, and likewise for August pay, so he might have paid him £20,000 as soon as might be.

22. It was appointed that, forasmuch as there was much disorder on the Marches on [the] Scotland side, both in vain fortifications of some places and negligent looking to other forts, the Duke of Northumberland, General Warden thereof, should go down and view it and take order for it and return home with speed. Also a pay of £10,000 to go before him.

23. It was appointed that these bands of men of arms should go with me this progress:

Lord Treasurer	30	Earl of Pembroke	50
Lord Great Master	25	Lord Admiral	15
Lord Privy Seal	30	Lord Darcy	30
Duke of Suffolk	25	Lord Cobham	20
Earl of Warwick	25	Lord Warden	20
Earl of Rutland	15	Mr Vice-Chamberlain	15
Earl of Huntingdon	25	Mr Sadler	10
		Mr Sidney	10

26. It was appointed that Thomas Gresham should have paid him out of the money that came of my debts £7,000, for to pay £6,800 the last of the month, which he received the same night.

28. The same Thomas Gresham had £9,000 paid him toward the payment of £26,000 which the Fuggers required to be paid at the Paschal Mart. For he had taken by exchange from hence £5,000 and odd, and £10,000 he borrowed of the Schetz, and ten of Lazarus Tucker. So there was in the whole 25, of which was paid the last of April 14, so the[re] remain £11,000 and £9,000, which I now made over by exchange, which made £20,000 to pay the Fuggers with.

30. I received advertisement from Mr Pickering that the French king went from Saverne to Arromaches, which was yielded to him, thence to Limbourg and so toward Spires, his army to be about 20,000 footmen and 8,000 horsemen well-appointed, besides rascals. He had with him fifty pieces of artillery, of which were twenty-six cannons and six organs and great number of boats. From Limbourg – partly doubting Duke Maurice's meaning, partly for lack of victuals, and also because he had word that the regent's army, of

which were guides the Count of Egmont, Mons. de Rie, Martin van Rossem, and Duke of Holest, to the number of 16,000 footmen and 6,000 horsemen, had invaded Champagne and fortified Aschenay – he retired homeward till he came to Striolph and there commanded all unprofitable carriage[s] and men should depart to Chalons, and sent to the Admiral to come to him with 6,000 Swiss, 4,000 Frenchmen, 1,500 horsemen, and thirty pieces of ordnance, meaning as it was thought to do some enterprise about Luxemburg, or to recover Aschenay, which the regent had fortified. There died in this journey 2,000 men for lack of good victuals. For eight days they had but bread and water, and they had marched sixty Dutch miles at the least and passed many a strait very painfully and laborsomely.

19. Duke Maurice, coming from Augsburg in great haste, came this day to the first passage, called the Clouse, which the emperor had caused to be strongly fortified and victualed, a passage through a hill, cut out artificially on the way to Innsbruck, and there was a strong bulwark made hard by it which he won, after a long fight, within an hour and a half by assault and took and slew all that were within; and that night he marched through that hill into a plain where he looked for to see twelve ensigns of landsknechts of his enemies. But they retired to the second strait, and yet divers of them were both slain and taken; and so that night he lodged in the plain at the entry of the second passage where were five forts and one castle, which with ordnance slew some of Duke Maurice's men.

20. This morning the Duke of Mecklenburg, with three thousand footmen, cast a bridge over a river five miles beneath [a] sluice and came and gave assault behind the sluice, and Duke Maurice gave assault in the face, and the countrymen of Tyrol, for hate of the Spaniards, help[ed] Duke Maurice, so that the five forts were won by assault and the castle yielded upon condition to depart, not to serve in three months after the emperor. In this enterprise he slew and took 3,500 persons and twenty-three pieces of artillery and 240,000 s[cutes]. The emperor, hearing of this, departed by night from Innsbruck forty miles that night in post; he killed two of his jennets and rode continually every night; first to Brixenium and after, for doubt of the Cardinal of Ferrara's army, turned to Villach in Carinthia the thirtieth of May, tarrying for the Duke of Alva, who should come to him with 2,000 Spaniards and 3,000 Italians that came from Parma. Also the emperor delivered Duke Frederick from captivity, and sent him through Bohemia into Saxony to raise a power against Duke Maurice, his nephew.

22. Duke Maurice, after that Hala and divers other towns about Innsbruck in Tyrol had yielded, came to Innsbruck and there caused all the stuff to be brought to the market place and took all that pertained to Imperialists as con-fiscate; the rest he suffered the townsmen to enjoy. He took there fifty pieces of ordnance, which he conveyed to Augsburg, for that town he fortified and made it his staple of provision.

JUNE

2. Sir John Williams, who was committed to the Fleet for disobeying a commandment given to him for not paying any pensions without making my Council privy, upon his submission was delivered out of prison.

4. Beaumont, M[aste]r of the Rolls, did confess his offenses, how in his office of wards he had bought land with my money, had lent it, and kept it from me to the [value of] £9,000 and above, more than this twelvemonth, and £11,000 in obligations, how, he being judge in the Chancery between the Duke of Suffolk and the Lady Powis, took her title and went about to get it into his hands, paying a sum [of] money and letting her have a farm of a manor of his and caused an indenture to be made falsely with the old duke's counterfeit hand to it, by which he gave these lands to the Lady Powis and went about to make twelve men perjured. Also how he had con-cealed the felony of his man, to the sum of £200 which he stole from him, taking the money to his own hand again. For these considerations he sur-rendered into my hands all his offices, lands, and goods movable and un-movable, toward the payment of this debt and of the fines due to these particular faults by him done.

6. The Lord Paget, Chancellor of the Duchy [of Lancaster], confessed how he, without commission, did sell away my lands and great timber woods; how he had taken great fines of my lands to his said peculiar profit and advantage, never turning any to my use or commodity; how he made leases in reversion for more than twenty-one years. For these crimes and other like recited before, he surrendered his office and submitted himself to those fines that I or my Council would appoint, to be levied of his goods and lands.

7. Whalley, Receiver of Yorkshire, confessed how he lent my money upon gain and lucre; how he paid one year's revenue over with the arrearages of the last; how he bought my own land with my money; how in his accounts he had made many false suggestions; how at the time of the fall of money he

borrowed divers sums of money and had allowance for it after, by which he gained £500 at one crying down, the whole sum being £2,000 and above. For these and suchlike considerations he surrendered his office and sub mitted to fines which I or my Council should assign him, to be levied of his goods and lands.

8. The Lords of the Council sat at Guildhall in London, where in the presence of a thousand people they declared to the mayor and brethren their slothfulness in suffering unreasonable prices of things, and to craftsmen their willfulness, etc., telling them that if upon this admonition they did not amend, I was wholly determined to call in their liberties as confiscate and to appoint officers that should look to them.

10. It was appointed that the Lord Grey of Wilton should be pardoned of his offenses and delivered out of the Tower.

Whereas Sir Philip Hoby should have gone to Calais with Sir Richard Cotton and William Barnes, auditor, it was appointed [that] Sir Anthony St Leger, Sir Richard Cotton, and Thomas Mildmay should go thither, carrying with them £10,000 to be received out of the Exchequer.

Whereas it was agreed that there should be a pay now made to Ireland of £5,000, and then the money to be cried down, it was appointed that 3,000 weight which I had in the Tower should be carried thither and coined at 3 *denar.* fine, and that incontinent the coin should be cried down.

Also . . . of . . . tenes play should be shifted [?] to the porter's lodge.

12. Because Pirry tarried here for the bullion, William Williams, assay master, was put in his place to view the mines with Mr Brabazon or him who the deputy should appoint.

13. Bannister and Crane – the one for his large confession, the other because little matter appeared against him – were delivered out of the Tower.

16. The Lord Paget was brought into the Star Chamber and there declared effectuously his submission by word of mouth and delivered it in writing. Beaumont, who had before made his confession in writing, began to deny it again, but after being called before my Council, he did confess it again and there acknowledged a fine of his land and signed an obligation in surrender of all his goods.

17. Mons. de Courrières took his leave.

2. The French king won the castle of Rodemanche.

3. Certain horsemen of the regent's came and set upon the French king's baggage and slew divers of the carters, but at length with some loss of the

Frenchmen they were compelled to retire. The French king won Mount Saint Jean.

4. The French king came to Damvillers, which was a strong town, and besieged it, making three breaches.

12. The town was yielded to him, with the captain. He found in it 2,500 footmen, 200 horsemen, 63 brass great-pieces, 300 harquebuses à croc, much victuals, and much munitions, as he did write to his ambassador.

19. It was appointed that the Bishop of Durham's matter should stay till the end of the progress.

20. Beaumont in the Star Chamber confessed, after a little sticking upon the matter, his faults, to which he had put to his hand.

23. It was agreed that the bands of men of arms appointed to Mr Sidney, Mr Vice-Chamberlain, Mr Hoby, and Mr Sadler should not be furnished but left off.

25. It was agreed that none of my Council should move me in any suit of land – for forfeits above £20, for reversions of leases, or any other extraordinary suits – till the state of my revenues were further known.

15. The French king came to a town standing on the river of Meuse called Yvoix, which gave him many hot skirmishes.

18. The French king began his battery to the walls.

14. The townsmen of Montmédy gave a hot skirmish to the French and slew Mons. de Toge's brother and many other gentlemen of the camp.

12. The Prince of Salerno, who had been with the French king to treat with him touching the matters of Naples, was dispatched in post with this answer: that the French king would aid him with 13,000 footmen and 1,500 horsemen, in the French wages, to recover and conquer the Kingdom of Naples, and he should marry, as some said, the French king's sister, Madam Marguerite. The cause why this prince rebelled against the emperor was partly the uncourteous handling of the Viceroy of Naples, partly ambition.

18. The Flemings made an invasion into Champagne, insomuch that the Dauphin had almost been taken, and the Queen, lying at Chalons, sent some of her stuff toward Paris.

12. Also another company took the town of Guise and spoiled the country also.

22. Mons. de Taille was [sent] for to raise the arrear bands and legionnaires of Picardy and Champagne, to recover Guise and invade Flanders.

27. Removing to Hampton Court.

42. *A fine State portrait of Lady Jane Grey. A simple and unaffected character who strongly disliked pomp and formality, she became a victim of Northumberland's bid for power after Edward's death.*

JANE GREY

Lady Jane Grey, while not a Tudor monarch, survives in history as the 'Nine Day Queen'. She was born in 1537, daughter of Henry Grey (later Duke of Suffolk) and Frances Brandon, a niece of Henry VIII. Her tragedy was to fall under the influence of the Duke of Northumberland, the most powerful man in England during Edward VI's last years. Northumberland sought to use Jane's proximity to the throne to perpetuate his own power and married her to his youngest son Guildford Dudley. He persuaded Edward to set aside Henry VIII's will and devolve the succession on Lady Jane as a Protestant claimant. Hence, after Edward's death, she was proclaimed queen on 10 July 1553.

Her 'reign' was brief. Northumberland had no popular support and there was no resistance to Mary when she entered the capital. Northumberland was executed and Jane imprisoned. Subsequently, after her father supported Thomas Wyatt's rebellion, Jane was beheaded, together with her father and her husband.

Jane was sixteen when she was executed. In the plotting which brought her so near the throne, and then to her death, she had no part. She made no enemies, and was, in the eyes of those who knew her, virtuous, gentle and guiltless.

From *The Schoolmaster* by Roger Ascham

Roger Ascham was a Cambridge scholar, a tutor to the future Queen Elizabeth and one of the foremost teachers of his age. In his celebrated work, The Schoolmaster, *he records an account of a conversation with Lady Jane Grey.*

'I will tell you, and tell you a truth, which perchance you will marvel at. One of the greatest benefits that ever God gave me is, that he sent me so sharp and severe parents, and so gentle a schoolmaster. For when I am in presence either of father or mother, whether I speak, keep silence, sit, stand or go; eat, drink, be merry or sad; be sewing, playing, dancing, or doing any thing else, I must do it, as it were in such weight, measure and number, even so perfectly, as God made the world, or else I am so sharply taunted, so cruelly threatened, yea presently sometimes with pinches, nips and bobs, and other ways which I will not name, for the honour I bear them, so without measure misordered, that I think myself in hell, till time come that I must go to Mr Elmer, who teacheth me so gently, so pleasantly, with such fair allurements to learning, that I think all the time nothing while I am with him. And when I am called from him I fall on weeping, because whatsoever else I do but learning, is full of grief, trouble, fear, and whole misliking unto me. And thus my book hath been so much my pleasure and bringeth daily to me more pleasure and more, that in respect of it, all other pleasures, in very deed, be but trifles and troubles unto me.'

From *A Harbour for Faithful Subjects* by John Aylmer

Dr Aylmer, or Elmer, was Lady Jane Grey's tutor and later, in the reign of Elizabeth, became Bishop of London. In his book, A Harbour for Faithful Subjects, *he gives this glowing character sketch of his pupil.*

The king left her rich cloths and jewels; and I know it to be true, that in seven years after her father's death, she never in all that time looked upon that rich attire and precious jewels but once, and that against her will. And that there never came gold or stone upon her head, till her sister forced her to lay off her former soberness, and bear her company in her glittering gayness. And then she so wore it, as every man might see that her body carried that which her heart misliked. I am sure that her maidenly apparel which she used in King Edward's time, made the noblemen's daughters and wives to be ashamed to be dressed and painted like peacocks; being more moved with her most virtuous example than with all that ever Paul or Peter wrote touching that matter. Yea, this I know, that a great man's daughter [Lady Jane Grey] receiving from Lady Mary before she was queen good apparel of tinsel, cloth of gold and velvet, laid on with parchment lace of gold, when she saw it, said; 'What shall I do with it?' 'Mary', said a gentlewoman, 'wear it.' 'Nay', quoth she, 'that were a shame, to follow my Lady Mary against God's word, and leave my Lady Elizabeth which followeth God's word.' And when all the ladies, at the coming of the Scots queen-dowager, went with their hair frownsed, curled and double curled, she altered nothing, but kept her old maidenly shamefacedness.

The Lady Jane Proclaimed Queen

The Lady Jane and Fecknam a Preist

The Lady Jane Beheaded in ỹ Tower

43. *A triptych summary of Lady Jane Grey's nine-day reign, from the same early history as the woodcut on page 57.*

44. *Mary Tudor, daughter of Henry VIII and Catherine of Aragon, whose reign was a determined attempt to reimpose her rigid Catholic faith on her subjects.*

MARY TUDOR

Mary's life story was one of almost unrelieved misery from the age of twelve when her mother, Queen Catherine, was cast off in favour of Anne Boleyn. Mary was forcibly separated from her mother, declared illegitimate, and urged to deny her Catholic faith. Despite all pressure, Mary showed pride and stubborness in resisting, and when she came to the throne it was with the object of restoring her people to Rome and remaining true to the memory of her mother.

The reign itself was disastrous. Mary's attempt to wipe out heresy by force not only failed but earned her the hatred of the people and the title 'Bloody Mary'. Her marriage to Philip of Spain was intensely unpopular, and her own love for her husband was in no way returned. Descriptions of Mary make it clear that she was physically unattractive and temperamentally withdrawn. Certainly Philip was not attracted, and spent most of the time abroad.

Mary to Henry VIII, 2 October 1533

After the birth of Elizabeth, Mary's status – even her entitlement to be called 'Princess' – was in question. This is her reply to an order to abandon her household at Beaulieu in Essex and to take up residence in Hertford Castle.

In most humble wise I beseech your grace of your daily blessing. Pleaseth the same to be advertised that this morning my chamberlain came and showed me that he had received a letter from Sir William Paulet, comptroller of your household; the effect whereof was that I should, with all diligence, remove to the Castle of Hertford. Where upon I desired him to see that letter, which he showed me, wherein was written that 'the Lady Mary, the king's daughter, should remove to the place aforesaid' – leaving out in the same the name of princess. Which, when I heard, I could not a little marvel, trusting verily that your grace was not privy to the same letter, as concerning the leaving out of the name of princess, forasmuch as I doubt not that your grace doth take me for your lawful daughter, born in true matrimony. Wherefore, if I were to say to the contrary, I should in my conscience run into the displeasure of God, which I hope assuredly that your grace would not that I should do.

And in all other things, your grace shall have me, always, as humble and

obedient daughter and handmaid as ever was child to the father, which my
duty bindeth me to, as knoweth our Lord, who have your grace in his most
holy tuition, with much honour and long life to his pleasure. By your most
humble daughter, Mary, *Princess*.

Eustace Chapuys to Charles V, 17 January 1534

*Eustace Chapuys was the Emperor Charles V's ambassador in London. Naturally
biased, he referred to the infant Elizabeth as the king's 'bastard daughter' and to Mary
as 'the Princess'. He lost no opportunity of telling anecdotes which reflected favourably
on Mary or adversely on Anne Boleyn, the king's 'amye'.*

The king lately went to see his bastard daughter, who is twenty miles away,
and the princess with her. Though one of the principal causes of his going
was to persuade or force the princess to renounce her title, when the lady
considered the king's easiness or lightness (if any one dared to call it so), and
that the beauty, virtue and prudence of the princess might assuage his wrath
and cause him to treat her better and leave her title, she sent Cromwell, and
then other messengers, after the king, to prevent him from seeing or speaking
with her. Accordingly, before arriving at the house, he sent orders that she
should not come to him. While in the house, and in the bastard's room, he
sent Cromwell, the treasurer and the captain of the guard, to urge the princess
to renounce her title. She replied that she had already given a decided answer;
it was labour wasted to press her, and they were deceived if they thought that
bad treatment or rudeness, or even the chance of death, would make her
change her determination.

While the king was with his new daughter, the princess sent to ask leave
to come and kiss his hand, but her request was not granted. When the king
was going to mount his horse she went on to a terrace at the top of the house
to see him. The king, either being told of it, or by chance, turned round, and
seeing her on her knees with her hands joined, bowed to her, and put his
hand to his hat. Then all those present, who had not dared to raise their heads
to look at her, rejoiced at what the king had done, and saluted her reverently
with signs of good will and compassion.

Eustace Chapuys to Charles V, 7 March 1534

When the king's 'amye' went lately to visit her daughter, she urgently solicited the princess to visit her and honour her as queen, saying that it would be a means of reconciliation with the king, and she herself (*ladite amitie*) would intercede with him for her, and she would be as well or better treated than ever. The princess replied that she knew no queen in England except her mother, and if the said 'amye' (whom she called Madame Anne de Bolans) would do her that favour with her father she would be obliged. The lady repeated her remonstrances and offers, and in the end threatened her, but could not move the princess. The other was very indignant, and intended to bring down the pride of the unbridled Spanish blood, as she said. She will do the worst she can.

'Concerning the Child-bed of Queen Mary' from Foxe's *Book of Martyrs*

Mary's greatest personal tragedy was her failure to produce a child. Near the end of her life she deceived herself that she was pregnant, mistaking the symptoms of the disease which was to kill her. In his Book of Martyrs, *Foxe describes the preparations made for the birth, though, as a good Protestant he viewed it as a ruse to provide the nation with a Catholic heir.*

Long persuasion had been in England, with great expectation, for the space of half a year or more, that the queen was conceived with child. This report was made by the queen's physicians, and others nigh about the Court; so that divers were punished for saying the contrary and commands were given that in all churches supplication and prayer should be made for the queen's good delivery, the certificate whereof you may read before in the letter of the Council sent to Bonner; and also the same moreover may appear by provision made before in Act of Parliament for the child.

And now forasmuch as in the beginning of this month of June, about Whitsuntide, the time was thought to be nigh that this young master should come into the world, and that midwives, rockers and nurses with the cradle and all were prepared and in readiness, suddenly, upon what cause or occasion it is uncertain, a certain vain rumour was blown in London of the

45. *Mary's ill-fated marriage to Philip II of Spain gave her a husband who returned none of her devotion, and who cared nothing for her country.*

prosperous deliverance of the queen and the birth of the child; insomuch that the bells were rung, bonfires and procession made, not only in the City of London and in most other parts of the realm, but also in the town of Antwerp guns were shot off upon the river by the English ships, and the marines thereof rewarded with a hundred pistolets or Italian crowns, by the lady regent who was the Queen of Hungary. Such great rejoicing and triumph was for the queen's delivery and that there was a prince born: yea, divers preachers, namely one the parson of St Anne within Aldergate, after procession and Te Deum sung, took it upon him to describe the proportion of the child, how fair, how beautiful, and great a prince it was, as the like had not been seen.

In the midst of this great ado, there was a simple man (this I speak but upon information) dwelling within four miles of Berwick, that never had been before half way to London, who said concerning the bonfires made for Queen Mary's child, 'Here is a joyful triumph but at length all will not prove worth a mess of pottage' – as indeed it came to pass. For in the end all proved clean contrary, and the joy and expectations of men were much deceived. For the people were certified that the queen neither was as then delivered, nor after was in hope to have any child.

At this time many talked diversly. Some said this rumour of the queen's conception was spread for a policy; some others affirmed that she was deceived by a tympany or some other like disease, to think herself with child, and was not; some thought she was with child, and that it did by some chance miscarry, or else that she was bewitched; but what was the truth thereof the Lord knoweth, to whom nothing is secret. One thing of mine own hearing and seeing I cannot pass over unwitnessed.

There came to me whom I did both hear and see, one Isabel Malt, a woman dwelling in Aldersgate street in Horn Alley, not far from the house where this present book was printed, who before witness made this declaration unto us, that she being delivered of a man-child upon Whitsunday in the morning, which was the 11th day of June 1555, there came to her the Lord North, and another lord of her unknown, dwelling then about Old fifthstreet, demanding of her if she would part with her child, and would swear that she ne'er knew nor had any such child. Which, if she would, her son (they said) would be well provided for, she should take no care for it, with many fair offers if she would part with the child.

After that came other women also, of whom, one they said should have been the rocker; but she in no wise would let go her son, who at the writing hereof being alive and called Timothy Malt, was of the age of thirteen years and upward.

Thus much I say, I heard from the woman herself. What credit is to be given to her relation, I deal not withal, but leave it to the liberty of the reader, to believe it they that list; to them that list not I have no further warrant to assure them.

Description by Giovanni Michele, 1557

Giovanni Michele, the Venetian ambassador in London, was another acute, if biased, observer of the English Court and wrote this description of Mary the year before her death.

She is of low stature, but has no deformity in any part of her person. She is thin and delicate, and altogether unlike her father, who was tall and strongly made, or her mother, who, although not tall, was stout. Her features are well formed, and, as her portraits prove, was considered, when younger, not merely good-looking but more than moderately pretty. At present, with the exception of some wrinkles, caused more by sorrow than by years, which make her appear older than in fact she is, her looks are of a grave and sedate cast. Her eyes are so piercing as to command not only respect but awe from those on whom she casts them, yet she is very nearsighted, being unable to read, or do anything else, without placing her eyes quite close to the object. Her voice is deep-toned, and rather masculine, so that when she speaks she is heard some distance off. In conclusion, she is a well-looking lady, nor, putting out of the question her rank as queen, should she ever be spoken ill of for want of sufficient beauty.

Extract from Mary's Last Will and Testament

With provision for the husband she adored and, in final pathos, for the 'issue between us', Mary's Will is an apt commentary on her unhappy reign.

And I do humbly beseech my said most dearest lord and husband to accept of my bequest and to keep for a memory of me one jewel, being a table diamond, which the emperor's majesty, his and my most honourable father, sent unto me by the Count d'Egmont, at the insurance of my said lord and husband, and also one other table diamond which his majesty sent unto me by the Marquis de les Nanes, and the collar of gold set with nine diamonds, the which his majesty gave me the Epiphany after our marriage, also the ruby now set in a gold ring, which his highness sent me by the Count of Feria, all which things I require his majesty to dispose of at his pleasure, and, if his highness think meet, to the issue between us.

46. *Mary as Queen: 'At present, with the exception of some wrinkles, caused more by sorrow than by years, which make her appear older than in fact she is, her looks are of a grave and sedate cast.'*

47. *A beautiful portrait of the young Elizabeth, from the Royal Collection, by an artist never identified.*

QUEEN ELIZABETH

Elizabeth's private life has been the cause of much speculation. Why, against all expectation and probability, did she never marry? Letters to her suitors, such as Eric of Sweden and Anjou of France, give few clues. They show her as a master of tact, demonstrate that she was prepared to use the prospect of marriage for diplomatic ends, but reveal little about the inner working of her mind.

In all probability the answer is a simple one: she enjoyed being queen, and realized that marriage would mean sharing – or, worse, giving up – her regal power. That is not to say she was unemotional; but on those occasions where it appeared that her heart would rule her head – her relationships with Dudley, and, near the end, Essex – it was, in the event, the heart which took second place.

Elizabeth, though often thought of as masculine, had her full measure of feminine characteristics. If she would never be won, she liked to be wooed, and could not stand the thought of any of her favourites finding attraction elsewhere. She found it hard to come to decisions, her vacillations driving her counsellors near despair. She hated the idea of growing old: John Harington, her godson, gives a remarkable picture of her in old age, in the aftermath of Essex's insubordinate behaviour and final treachery.

The queen's personality did much to shape her age. Her early life had taught her the lessons of a politique, how to adjust to, and survive, such different régimes as those of her father, half-brother and half-sister. Always she preferred compromises to conflict, and so her policies tended to steer a middle course as long as possible. Thus her religious policy, foreign policy, her relations with Parliament – and with her suitors – were largely an extended theme of indecision. Yet there were good reasons for not aligning herself with the extremists who, from both sides, criticized the via media. In the end her conciliatory policies were triumphantly vindicated as she handed over the reins of a nation more united than had seemed possible to her successor, James VI of Scotland.

48. A court dance in the Elizabethan age.

Lady Bryan to Thomas Cromwell, 1536

Lady Margaret Bryan was Elizabeth's first governess. Shortly after the execution of Elizabeth's mother, Anne Boleyn, in May 1536, she wrote to the king's chief minister about the difficulties of maintaining a properly ordered household at Hunsdon.

My lord, when your lordship was last here, it pleased you to say that I should not mistrust the king's grace nor your lordship, which word was more comfort to me than I can write, as God knoweth. And now it emboldens me to show you my poor mind. My lord, when my Lady Mary's grace was born, it pleased the king's grace to appoint me lady-mistress and made me a baroness. And so I have been governess to the children his grace have had since.

Now it is so, my Lady Elizabeth is put from that degree she was afore, and what degree she is of now, I know not but by hearsay. Therefore I know not how to order her, nor myself, nor none of hers that I have the rule of – that is her women and grooms, beseeching you to be good lord to my lady, and to all hers: and that she may have some raiment; for she hath neither gown, nor kirtle [slip], nor petticoat, nor no manner of linen nor smocks, nor kerchiefs, nor rails [nightdresses], nor body stitchets [corsets], nor biggens [night-caps]. All these her grace must take I have driven off as long as I can, that by my troth I can drive it off no longer: beseeching you my lord, that ye will see that her grace may have that which is needful for her, as my trust is that ye will do. Beseeching ye, mine own good lord, that I may know from you what is the king's grace's pleasure and yours; that I shall do in everything? And what-soever it shall please the king's grace or your lordship to command me at all times, I shall fulfil it to the best of my power.

My lord, Mr Shelton saith he is master of this house. What fashion that may be I cannot tell, for I have not seen it afore. My lord, ye be so honourable yourself, and every man reporteth that your lordship loveth honour, that I trust you will see the house honourably ordered, as it ever hath been aforetime. And if it please you that I may know what your order is, and if it be not performed I shall certify your lordship of it. For I fear me it will be hardly enough performed. But if the head [Shelton] knew what honour meaneth, it will be the better ordered – if not, it will be hard to bring to pass.

My lord, Mr Shelton would have my Lady Elizabeth to dine and sup every day at the board of estate. Alas! my lord, it is not meet for a child of her age to keep such rule yet. I promise you, my lord, I dare not take it upon me to keep her grace in health an' she keep that rule. For there she shall see divers meats, and fruits, and wine, which it would be hard for me to restrain her grace from. Ye know, my lord, there is place of correction there; and she is yet too young to correct greatly. I know well an' she be there, I shall neither bring her up to the king's grace's honour, nor hers, nor to her health, nor to my poor honesty. Wherefore, I show your lordship this my desire, beseeching you, my lord, that my lady may have a mess of meat at her own lodging, with a good or two that is meet of her grace to eat of; and the reversion of the mess shall satisfy all her women, a gentleman usher, and a groom; which be eleven persons on her side. Sure I am it will be as great profit to the king's grace this way as the other way. For if all this should be set abroad, they must have three or four messes of meat – whereas this one mess shall suffice them all with bread and drink, according as my Lady Mary's grace had afore, and to be ordered in all things as her grace was afore.

God knoweth my lady [Elizabeth] hath great pain with her great teeth, and they come very slowly forth, which causeth me to suffer her grace to have her will more than I would. I trust to God an' her teeth were well graft, to have her grace after another fashion than she is yet: so as I trust the king's grace shall have great comfort in her grace. For she is as toward a child and as gentle of conditions, as ever I knew any in my life. Jesu preserve her grace!

As for a day or two, at a high time, or whensoever it shall please the king's grace to have her set abroad, I trust so to the king's honour and hers; and then after to take her ease again . . .

From Hundson, with the evil hand of her who is your daily bead-woman, MARGT. BRYAN.

49. Elizabeth's dedication to Katherine Parr of her own translation of The Queen's Prayers and Meditations. Both her script and her Italian attest the high standard of her education as convincingly as does Roger Ascham.

ORATIONI, O VERO ME ditationi dalle quali la mente c'incitata a patientemente pa- tire ogni afflittione, et sprezzare la vana prosperita di questo mō- do, et sempre desiderare l'eterna beatitudine: raccolte da alcune sante opere, per la valorossima, et humanissima princessa, Cathe- rina reina d'inghilterra, francia et hibernia. Tradotte per la signo- ra Elizabetta dalla lingua inglese in vulgare italiano.

50. *A late portrait of Katherine Parr, Henry VIII's widow, who married again into the Seymour family and survived to die a natural death.*

Elizabeth to Katherine Parr, 31 July 1544

This is the earliest surviving letter written by Elizabeth (in Italian) when she was in her eleventh year.

Inimical fortune, envious of all good and ever revolving human affairs, has deprived me for a whole year of your most illustrious presence, and, not thus content, has yet again robbed me of the same good; which thing would be intolerable to me, did I not hope to enjoy it very soon. And in this my exile I well know that the clemency of your highness has had as much care and solicitude for my health as the king's majesty himself. By which thing I am not only bound to serve you, but also to revere you with filial love, since I understand that your most illustrious highness has not forgotten me every time you have written to the king's majesty, which, indeed, it was my duty to have requested from you. For heretofore I have not dared to write to him. Wherefore I now humbly pray your most excellent highness, that, when you write to his majesty, you will condescend to recommend me to him, praying ever for his sweet benediction, and similarly entreating our Lord God to send him best success, and the obtaining of victory over his enemies, so that your highness and I may, as soon as possible, rejoice together with him on his happy return. No less pray I God, that He would preserve your most illustrious highness; to Whose grace, humbly kissing your hands, I offer and recommend myself.

From St James's this 31st July.

Your most obedient daughter, and most faithful servant,

ELIZABETH.

Elizabeth to Edward VI, 1550

This letter was sent with a present of her portrait, and is prudently fulsome in its sentiments towards her half-brother.

Like as the rich man that daily gathereth riches to riches, and to one bag of money layeth a great sort till it come to infinite: so methinks your majesty, not being sufficed with so many benefits and gentleness shewed to me afore this time, doth now increase them in asking and desiring where you may bid and command; requiring a thing not worthy the desiring for itself, but made worthy for your highness' request. My picture I mean: in which, if the inward good mind toward your grace might as well be declared as the outward face and countenance shall be seen, I would not have tarried the commandment but prevented it, nor have been the last to grant but the first to offer it. For the face I grant I might well blush to offer, but the mind I shall never be ashamed to present. But though from the grace of the picture the colours may fade by time, may give by weather, may be spited by chance; yet the other, nor time with her swift wings shall overtake, nor the misty clouds with their lowering may darken, nor chance with her slippery foot may overthrow.

Of this also yet the proof could not be great, because the occasions have been so small; notwithstanding, as a dog hath a day, so may I perchance have time to declare it in deeds, which now I do write them but in words. And further, I shall humbly beseech your majesty, that when you shall look on my picture, you will vouchsafe to think, that as you have but the outward shadow of the body afore you, so my inward mind wisheth that the body itself were oftener in your presence. Howbeit because both my so being I think could do your majesty little pleasure, though myself great good; and again, because I see not as yet the time agreeing thereunto, I shall learn to follow this saying of Horace, 'Feras, non culpes, quod vitari non potest'. And thus I will (troubling your majesty I fear) end with my most humble thanks; beseeching God long to preserve you to his honour, to your comfort, to the realm's profit and to my joy.

From Hatfield this 15th day of May.

Your majesty's most humble sister and servant
ELIZABETH

Elizabeth to Queen Mary, 16 March 1554

A letter written when Elizabeth was ordered to the Tower on suspicion of being involved in the rebellion, primarily against the queen's Spanish marriage, led by Thomas Wyatt.

If any ever did try this old saying, 'that a king's word was more than another man's oath', I most humbly beseech your majesty to verify it to me, and to remember your last promise and my last demand, that I be not condemned without answer and due proof, which it seems that I now am; for without cause proved, I am by your Council from you commanded to go to the

If any ever did try this olde sayenge that a kinges worde was more tha
a nother mans othe, I most humbly beseche your M. to verefie it in
me and to remember your last promis and my last demaunde that I
be not condemned without answer and due profe wiche it semes that now I am for
that without cause provid I am by your counsel frome you comanded
to go vnto the tower a place more wonted for a false traitor, tha a tru
subiect wiche thogth I knowe I deserue it not, yet in the face of
al this realme apperes that it is provid wiche I pray god I may dy the
shamefullist dethe that euer any died afore I may mene any suche
thinge and to this present hower I protest afor God (who shal iuge
my trueth whatsoeuer malice shal denis) that I neuer practised
conciled nor cosented to any thinge that micth be preiudicial
to your parson any way or dangerous to the state by any
mene And therfor I humbly beseche your maiestie to let
me answer afore your selfe and not suffer me to trust your
counselors yea and that afore I go to the tower (if it
be possible) if not afor I be further condemned, howbeit I
trust assuredly your highnes wyl giue me leue to do it afore I go
for that thus shamfully I may not be cried out on as now I shal
be, yea and without cause. let consciens moue your hithnes to
take some bettar way with me tha to make me be condemned
in al mes sigth afor my desert knowen. Also I most humbly
beseche your highnes to pardon this my boldnes wiche
innocency procures me to do toother with hope of your natural
kindnis wiche I trust wyl not se me cast away without desert
wiche what it is I wold desier no more of God but that you
truly knewe. Wiche thinge I thinke and beleue you shal
neuer by report knowe vnles by your selfe you hire. I haue
harde in my time of many cast away for want of comminge
to the presence of ther prince and in late days I harde my
lorde of Somerset say that if his brother had bine suffered
to speke with him he had neuer suffered but the
persuasions wer made to him so gret that he was brogth
in belefe that he coulde not liue safely if the admiral liued
and that made him giue his consent to his dethe thogth
thes parsons ar not to be copared to your maiestie yet I
pray god as euel persuasions persuade not one sistar agains
the other and al for that the haue harde false report and
not harkene to the trueth knowen

therfor, ons agam with humblenes of my hart, bicause I am not
suffered to bow the knees of my body I humbly crave to speke
with your highthms wiche I wolde not be so bold to desier
if I knewe not my selfe most clere as I knowe my selfe most
tru. and as for the traitor Wiat he might paraventur writ
me a lettar but on my faithe I never receved any from him and
as for the copie of my lettar sent to the freche kinge I pra
God confound me eternally if ever I sent him word, message,
toke or lettar by any menes, and to this my truth
I will stande it my dethe.

I humbly crave but only one worde
of answer fro your selfe.

Your highnes most faithful subiett that
hathe bine from the beginninge and wylbe
to my ende . Elizabeth

(Continuation of letter from previous page.)

Tower, a place more wanted for a false traitor than a true subject, which though I know I desire it not, yet in the face of all this realm it appears proved. I pray to God I may die the shamefullest death that any ever died, if I may mean any such thing; and to this present hour I protest before God (Who shall judge my truth, whatsoever malice shall devise), that I never practised, counselled, nor consented to anything that might be prejudicial to your person any way, or dangerous to the state by any means. And therefore I humbly beseech your majesty to let me answer afore yourself, and not suffer me to trust to your councillors, yea, and that afore I go to the Tower, if it be possible; if not, before I be further condemned. Howbeit, I trust assuredly your highness will give me leave to do it afore I go, that thus shamefully I may not be cried out on, as I now shall be; yea, and that without cause. Let conscience move your highness to pardon this my boldness, which innocency procures me to do, together with hope of your natural kindness, which I trust will not see me cast away without desert, which what it is I would desire no more of God but that you truly knew. Which thing I think and believe you shall never by report know, unless by yourself you hear. I have heard in my time of many cast away for want of coming to the presence of their prince; and in late days I heard my Lord of Somerset say that if his brother had been suffered to speak with him he had never suffered; but persuasions were made to him so great that he was brought in belief that he could not live safely if the Admiral lived, and that made him give consent to his death. Though these persons are not to be compared to your majesty, yet I pray God the like evil persuasions persuade not one sister against the other, and all for that they have heard false report, and the truth not known. Therefore, once again, kneeling with humbleness of heart, because I am not suffered to bow the knees of my body, I humbly crave to speak with your highness, which I would not be so bold as to desire if I knew not myself most clear, as I know myself most true. And as for the traitor Wyatt, he might peradventure write me a letter, but on my faith I never received any from him. And as for the copy of the letter sent to the French king, I pray God confound me eternally if ever I sent him word, message, token, or letter, by any means, and to this truth I will stand in till my death.

Your highness's most faithful subject, that hath been from the beginning, and will be to my end,

ELIZABETH

I humbly crave but only one word of answer from yourself.

From *The Schoolmaster* by Roger Ascham

Elizabeth's high standard of education and her many accomplishments are recorded in this extract from the famous work by her tutor.

Numberless honourable ladies of the present time surpass the daughters of Sir Thomas More in every kind of learning. But amongst them all, my illustrious mistress the Lady Elizabeth shines like a star, excelling them more by the splendour of her virtues and her learning than by the glory of her royal birth. In the variety of her commendable qualities, I am less perplexed to find matter for the highest panegyric than to circumscribe that panegyric within just bounds. Yet I shall mention nothing respecting her but what has come under my own observation.

For two years she pursued the study of Greek and Latin under my tuition; but the foundations of her knowledge in both languages were laid by the diligent instruction of William Grindal, my late beloved friend, and seven years my pupil in classical learning at Cambridge. From this university he was summoned by John Cheke to Court, where he soon after received the appointment of tutor to this lady. After some years, when through her native genius, aided by the efforts of so excellent a master, she had made a great progress in learning; and Grindal by his merit and the favour of his mistress, might have aspired to high dignities; he was snatched away by a sudden illness, leaving a greater miss of himself in the Court, than I remember any other to have done these many years.

I was appointed to succeed him in his office; and the work which he had so happily begun, without my assistance indeed, but not without some counsels of mine, I diligently laboured to complete. Now, however, released from the throng of a Court, and restored to the felicity of my former learned leisure, I enjoy, through the bounty of the king, an honourable appointment in this university.

The Lady Elizabeth has accomplished her sixteenth year; and so much solidity of understanding, such courtesy united with dignity, have never been observed at so early an age. She has the most ardent love of true religion and of the best kind of literature. The constitution of her mind is exempt from female weakness, and she is endued with a masculine power of application. No apprehension can be quicker than hers, no memory more retentive. French and Italian she speaks like English; Latin, with fluency, propriety and judgment; she also spoke Greek with me, frequently, willingly, and moderately well. Nothing can be more elegant than her handwriting, whether in the Greek or Roman character. In music she is very skilful, but does not greatly delight. With respect to personal decoration, she greatly prefers a simple elegance to show and splendour, so despising 'the outward adorning of plaiting the hair and of wearing of gold', that in the whole manner of her life she rather resembles Hippolyta than Phaedra.

She read with me almost the whole of Cicero and a great part of Livy: from these two authors, indeed, her knowledge of the Latin language has been almost exclusively derived. The beginning of the day was always devoted by her to the New Testament in Greek, after which she read select orations of Isocrates and the tragedies of Sophocles, which I judged best adapted to supply her tongue with the purest diction, her mind with the most excellent precepts, and her exalted station with a defence against the utmost power of fortune. For her religious instruction, she drew first from the fountains of Scripture; and afterwards from St Cyprian, the 'Common places' of Melancthon and similar works which convey pure doctrine in elegant language. In every kind of writing she easily detected any ill-adapted or far-fetched expression. She could not bear those feeble imitators of Erasmus who bind the Latin language in the fetters of miserable proverbs; on the other hand, she approved a style chaste in its propriety and beautiful by perspicuity: and she greatly admired metaphors when not too violent, and antitheses when just and happily opposed. By a diligent attention to these particulars, her ears became so practised and so nice, that there was nothing in Greek, Latin, or English, prose or verse, which, according to its merits or its defects, she did not either reject with disgust, or receive with the highest delight . . .

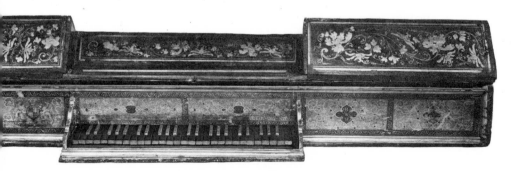

52. *Queen Elizabeth's virginals. The Queen was a very capable performer from an early age.*

Elizabeth to Eric, King of Sweden, 25 February 1560

*In the period following her accession Elizabeth was courted by numerous suitors.
All were discarded – some less rapidly than others for diplomatic reasons. Among the
most persistent, but most quickly rejected, was Eric, King of Sweden.*

Most Serene Prince, our very dear Cousin,
A letter truly yours both in the writing and sentiment, was given us on
30 December by your very dear brother, the Duke of Finland. And while
we perceive therefrom that the zeal and love of your mind towards us is not
diminished, yet in part we are grieved that we cannot gratify your serene
highness with the same kind of affection. And that indeed does not happen
because we doubt in any way of your love and honour, but, as often we have
testified both in words and in writing, that we have never yet conceived a
feeling of that kind of affection towards any one. We therefore beg your
serene highness again and again that you be pleased to set a limit to your love,
that it advance not beyond the laws of friendship for the present nor disregard
them in the future. And we in our turn shall take care that, whatever can be
required for the holy preservation of friendship between princes, we will
always perform towards your serene highness. It seems strange for your
serene highness to write that you understand from your brother and your
ambassadors that we have entirely determined not to marry an absent husband;
and that we will give you no certain reply until we shall have seen your
person . . . we have often given the same answer that we certainly think that
if God ever direct our heart to consideration of marriage, we shall never
accept or choose any absent husband, how powerful and wealthy a prince
soever. But that we are not to give you an answer until we have seen your
person is so far from the thing itself that we never even considered such a
thing. But I have always given both to your brother, who is certainly a most
excellent prince and deservedly very dear to us, and also to your ambassador
likewise, the same answer with scarcely any variation of the words, that we
do not conceive in our heart to take a husband but highly commend this
single life, and hope that your serene highness will not longer spend time in
waiting for us. But we will not greatly reprehend those things in your letter,
nor will we blame your brother or your ambassadors, since it can come to
pass that either your mind may gladly think these things, or has given ear to

one telling the like, so that what the mind greatly wishes, as often happens, it thinks to be true. Your most noble brother in this cause has certainly been always so insistent, and with such ready will and eager zeal has pursued it, that for himself he could not have shown more anxious care. Such indeed was his constancy in labouring and his skill in persuasion, that had your serene highness been present, nothing, as we think, would have been added to his zeal or carefulness or counsel or advice. We write thus with our own hand and mind, without summoning any to our counsel, because I understand that such is your serene highness' wish. What indeed appertains to all the remaining duties of humanity and kindness, that can be pleasing to your serene highness, or convenient and safe for the subjects of us both, we will never omit. God keep your serene highness for many years in good health and safety . . .

Your serene highness' sister and cousin,
ELIZABETH

Concerning your coming, however earnest your desire, yet we dare not approve the plan. Since nothing but expectation can happen to your serene highness in this business, and indeed we very greatly fear lest your love, which is now so great, might be turned to another and alien feeling, which would not be so pleasing to your serene highness, and to us also would be very grievous.

53. Before his swift rejection from her favours, Elizabeth had dispatched the artist Van der Meulen to paint this likeness of Eric of Sweden. He must have liked it more than she: he rewarded the artist with an extra payment.

An Encounter with the Dean of St Paul's, 1561

Though not averse to some aspects of Church ceremony, Elizabeth had no liking for 'popish' images. This anecdote is recorded in Nicholls's Progresses of Queen Elizabeth.

The aforesaid dean [Nowell] so often noted for his frequent preaching before the queen, and in other great and honourable assemblies, preached on the festival of the Circumcision, being New Year's day, at St Paul's, whither the queen resorted. Here a remarkable passage happened, as is recorded in a great man's memorials, who lived in those times. The dean, having gotten from a foreigner several fine cuts and pictures representing the stories and passions of the saints and martyrs, had placed them against the Epistles and Gospels of their festivals in a Common Prayer Book; and this book he had caused to be richly bound and laid on the cushion for the queen's use, in the place where she commonly sat, intending it for a New Year's gift to her majesty, and thinking to have pleased her fancy therewith. But it had not that effect, but the contrary: for she considered how this varied from her late open injunctions and proclamations against the superstitious use of images in churches: and for the taking away all such relics of popery. When she came to her place, she opened the book and perused it, and saw the pictures; but frowned and blushed, and then shut it (of which several took notice); and, calling the verger, bad him bring her the old book, wherein she was formerly wont to read. After sermon, whereas she was wont to get immediately on horseback, or into her chariot, she went straight to the vestry, and applying herself to the dean, thus she spoke to him:

Q. Mr Dean, how came it to pass that a new service-book was placed on my cushion?

To which the Dean answered:

D. May it please your majesty, I caused it to be placed there.

Then said the queen:

Q. Wherefore did you so?

D. To present your majesty with a New Year's gift.

Q. You could never present me with a worse.

D. Why so, Madam?

Q. You know I have an aversion to idolatry, to images and pictures of this kind.

D. Wherein is the idolatry, may it please your majesty?

Q. In the cuts resembling angels and saints; nay, grosser absurdities, pictures resembling the Blessed Trinity.

D. I meant no harm: nor did I think it would offend your majesty when I intended it for a New Year's gift.

Q. You must needs be ignorant then. Have you forgot our proclamation against images, pictures, and Romish relics in the churches? Was it, not read in your deanery?

D. It was read. But be your majesty assured, I meant no harm, when I caused the cuts to be bound with the service-book.

Q. You must needs be very ignorant to do this after our prohibition of them.

D. It being my ignorance, your majesty may the better pardon me.

Q. I am sorry for it: yet glad to hear it was your ignorance, rather than your opinion.

D. Be your majesty assured, it was my ignorance.

Q. If so, Mr Dean, God grant you his spirit, and more wisdom for the future.

D. Amen, I pray God.

Q. I pray, Mr Dean, how came you to these pictures? Who engraved them?

D. I know not who engraved them. I bought them.

Q. From whom bought you them?

D. From a German.

Q. It is well it was from a stranger. Had it been any of our subjects, we should have questioned the matter. Pray let no more of these mistakes, or of this kind, be committed within the churches of our realm for the future.

D. There shall not.

54. *Nowell, Dean of St Paul's.*

55. *A portrait by Zuccaro of Queen Elizabeth which gives a glimpse of the Court seen in the colonnaded corridor behind her.*

Melville at the English Court, 1564

Sir James Melville of Halhill was a Scottish envoy and traveller who was employed on various missions by a number of European rulers. His first visit to London was with the object of showing a portrait of Duke Casimir (son of the Elector Palatine and one of Elizabeth's suitors) to the queen. He recorded a number of impressions, including the lively interest displayed by Elizabeth in comparing her own attributes with those of the young Queen of Scots.

She appeared to be so affectionate to the queen her good sister that she had a great desire to see her. And because their desired meeting could not be so hastily brought to pass, she delighted to look upon her majesty's picture. She took me to her bed-chamber and opened a little desk, wherein were divers little pictures wrapt within paper, and their names written with her own hand upon the papers. Upon the first that she took up was written, 'My lord's picture'. I held the candle, and pressed to see that picture so named. She was loath to let me see it; at length my importunity prevailed for a sight thereof and found it to be the Earl of Leicester's picture. I desired that I might have it to carry home to my queen; which she refused, alleging that she had but that one picture of his. I said again that she had the original; for he was at the farthest part of the chamber, speaking with secretary Cecil. Then she took out the queen's picture, and kissed it; and I kissed her hand, for the great love I saw she bore to my mistress. She showed me also a fair ruby, as great as a tennis-ball. I desired that she would either send it or else my Lord of Leicester's picture, as a token unto the queen. She said, if the queen would follow her counsel, that she would in process of time get them both, and all she had; but in the mean time she was resolved for a token to send her with me a diamond. It was at this time late after supper; she appointed me to be with her the next morning by eight hours, at which time she used to walk in her garden. She enquired several things of me relating to this king-dom [Scotland], and other countries wherein I had lately travelled. She caused me to dine with her dame of honour, my Lady Stafford (an honour-able and godly lady, who had been at Geneva banished during the reign of

56. *A miniature by Nicholas Hilliard of the Earl of Leicester.*

Queen Mary), that I might be always near her majesty, that she might confer with me . . .

At divers meetings there would be divers purposes. The queen my sovereign had instructed me to leave matters of gravity sometimes, and cast in merry purposes, lest otherwise I should be tired upon, she being well informed of her sister's natural temper. Therefore, in declaring the customs of Dutchland [Germany], Poland and Italy, the busking and clothing of the women was not forgot, and what country weed I thought best becoming gentlewomen. The Queen of England said she had clothes of every sort; which every day, so long as I was there, she changed. One day she had the English weed, another the French, and another the Italian, and so forth. She asked me which of them became her best. I said, the Italian dress; which pleased her well, for she delighted to shew her golden coloured hair, wearing a caul and bonnet as they do in Italy. Her hair was more reddish than yellow, curled in appearance naturally.

She desired to know of me what colour of hair was reputed best; and whether my queen's hair or hers was best; and which of them two was fairest. I answered that the fairness of them both was not their worst faults. But she was earnest with me to declare which of them I thought fairest. I said she was the fairest queen in England and ours the fairest queen in Scotland. Yet

57. *A gouache painting by an unkown artist showing Queen Elizabeth giving audience to two Dutch ambassadors: a vivid glimpse of the kind of scene described by Melville.*

58. *Queen Elizabeth's table clock.*

she was earnest. I answered they were both the fairest ladies of their courts and that her majesty was whiter, but our queen was very lovely. She enquired which of them was of highest stature. I said, our queen. Then, saith she, she is too high and that herself was neither too high nor too low. Then she asked what kind of exercises she used. I answered that when I was dispatched out of Scotland, the queen was lately come from the Highland hunting; that when she had leisure from the affairs of her country she read upon good books, the histories of diverse countries, and sometimes would play upon the lute and virginals. She asked if she played well. I said, reasonably for a queen.

That same day after dinner my Lord of Hunsdon drew me up to a quiet gallery, that I might hear some music (but he said he durst not avow it), where I might hear the queen play upon the virginals. After I had hearkened a while, I took by the tapestry that hung before the door of the chamber, and, seeing her back was towards the door, I entered within the chamber, and stood still at the door check and heard her play excellently well. But she left off as soon as she turned her about and saw me and came forward, seeming to strike me with her left hand and alleging that she used not to play before men, but when she was solitary, to shun melancholy. She asked how I came there. I said, 'As I was walking with my Lord of Hunsdon, as we passed by the chamber-door, I heard such melody as ravished me and drew me within the chamber, I knew not how'; excusing my fault of homeliness, as being brought up in the court of France, and was now willing to endure what kind of punishment her majesty should be pleased to lay upon me for my offence. Then she sat down low upon a cushion, and I upon my knees beside her; but she gave me a cushion with her own hand, to lay under my knee; which at first I refused, but she compelled me to take it. She then called for my Lady Stafford out of the next chamber; for the queen was alone. Then she asked

59. One of the grandest surviving portraits of Queen Elizabeth at the height of her powers, which well illustrates obvious enjoyment of fine cloth and jewellery.

whether my queen or she played best. In that I gave her the praise. She said my French was good, and asked if I could speak Italian, which she spoke reasonably well. I said I tarried not above two months in Italy and had brought with me some books to read upon, but had no time to learn the language perfectly. Then she spake to me in Dutch [German], which was not good; and would know what kind of books I liked best; whether of theology, history, or love matters. I said I liked well of all the sorts.

I was earnest to be despatched, but she said I was weary sooner of her company than she was of mine. I told her majesty that though I had no reason of being weary, it was time to return. But I was stayed two days longer, till I might see her dance, as I was informed. Which being done, she enquired of me whether she or my queen danced best. I answered that the queen danced not so high or disposedly as she did. Then again she wished that she might see the queen at some convenient place of meeting. I offered to convoy her secretly to Scotland by post, clothed like a page, disguised, that she might see that queen, as James V had gone in disguise to France with his own ambassador, to see the Duke of Vendôme's sister, who should have been his wife; telling her that her chamber might be kept in her absence as though she were sick, and in the meantime none to be privy thereto, except my Lady Stafford and one of the grooms of her chamber. She appeared to like that kind of language, and said, 'Alas, if I might do it.'

Elizabeth to Mary, Queen of Scots, 24 February 1567

Written shortly after Mary's husband, Lord Darnley, had been murdered, in this letter the angry tone of warning is thinly veiled.

Madam,
My ears have been so astounded and my heart so frightened to hear of the horrible and abominable murder of your husband and my own cousin that

A portrait by an unknown artist, in the Victoria and Albert Museum, Elizabeth's ever-present yet ever-... rival, Mary Stuart, Queen of ...s: while she was living she ... a constant potential focus of ...tholic discontent.

I have scarcely spirit to write: yet I cannot conceal that I grieve more for you than him. I should not do the office of a faithful cousin and friend, if I did not urge you to preserve your honour, rather than look through your fingers at revenge on those who have done you that pleasure as most people say. I counsel you so to take this matter to heart, that you may show the world what a noble princess and loyal woman you are. I write thus vehemently not that I doubt, but for affection. As for the three matters communicated by Melville, I understand your wish to please me, and that you will grant the request by Lord Bedford in my name to ratify the treaty made six or seven years past. On other things I will not trouble you at length, referring you to the report of this gentleman.

Elizabeth to George Talbot, Earl of Shrewsbury, and his wife, 4 June 1577

A light-hearted letter thanking the Earl and Countess of Shrewsbury for entertaining her favourite the Earl of Leicester, and offering them some advice about his eating habits.

Right Trusty,
Being given to understand from our cousin, the Earl of Leicester, how honourably he was lately received and used by you, our cousin the countess at Chatsworth, and how his diet is by you both discharged at Buxton, we should do him great wrong holding him in that place in our favour in which we do, in case we should not let you understand in how thankful sort we accept the same at both your hands, which we do not acknowledge to be done unto him to our self; and therefore do mean to take upon us the debt and to acknowledge you both as creditors so you can be content to accept us for debtor, wherein is the danger unless you cut off some part of the large allowance of diet you give him, lest otherwise the debt thereby may grow to be so great as we shall not be able to discharge the same, and so become bankrupt. And therefore we think it for the saving of our credit meet to prescribe unto you a proportion of diet which we mean in no case you shall exceed, and that is, to allow him by the day for his meat two ounces of flesh, referring the quality to yourselves, so as you exceed not the quantity, and for his drink the twentieth part of a pint of wine to comfort his stomach, and as much of St Anne's sacred water as he listeth to drink. On festival days, as is meet for a man of his quality, we can be content you shall enlarge his diet by

61. *Hoefnagel's drawing of one of the grand Tudor palaces around which Elizabethan Court life constantly revolved, Nonsuch Palace. Started by Henry VIII in 1538 as a rival to the Château de Chambord, it was destroyed in 1670, and nothing remains today but its foundations.*

allowing unto him for his dinner the shoulder of a wren, and for his supper a leg of the same, besides his ordinary ounces. The like proportion we mean you shall allow to our brother of Warwick, saving that we think it meet that in respect that his body is more replete than his brother's, that the wren's leg allowed at supper on festival days be abated, for that light supper agreeth best with rules of physic. This order our meaning is you shall inviolably observe, and so may you right well assure yourselves of a most thankful debtor to so well deserving a creditor.

Elizabeth to Francis, Duke of Anjou, 17 January 1580

This letter and the one following, promising much and meaning little, are typical of Elizabeth's letters to 'her frog'.

My excessive delay, my dearest, in not acknowledging the infinite ways in which my obligations on your behalf increase may render me rightly unworthy of treatment so honourable. But the extreme pain in my throat continually this past fortnight will have force, I hope, to blot out such a thought. And at this hour, finding myself a little better, I present my humblest thanks for having shown us a shining rock, against which neither the tempests of false persuasion nor the storm of evil tongues have ever had power to move the constancy of your affection, whereof I confess myself very unworthy for any perfection that I possess, and for that matter, which seems to me so much the more notable as the occasion is simpler. For one thing I rejoice, that you are so well furnished with good advice that you will not be ignorant of some of my defects so that I am assured of not being found worse than they already make me. And besides, being so well advised, you will be well resolved or you will not hazard it. And I pray to God to give you the gift of clear sight to penetrate the abysm of their subtleties and that I live not to be the means of your discontent. It is so difficult at this time to recognize the difference be- tween seeming and being, so that I wish that the wisdom of Solomon dwelt in your spirit to discern the counterfeit from the true, and such as look further instead of setting you up as the aim for their shafts. Those must be most highly thought of who respect us, but not with a mixture of their greatness and government. But at this moment I must as old women are wont in their dreams, not having slept well. I have received news from the king that the commissioners make themselves ready, but do not yet know that they are. I did not think before that France was so ill-furnished of princes and persons of great rank that they would be constrained to send me a child or man of low birth. I believe that they do it to lessen the greatness of my honour, or to cause impediments not to send at all. I have notwithstanding used roundness with the king, sending to tell him by his ambassador that I would not suffer a matter of so great weight to take any disgrace from the hate which is borne me. I have no mind to allow the chronicles to say that there will be an ill opinion of the makers of so great a feast, promising, I believe that the king will hold in honourable consideration both the place which you bear and the spirit with which I bear myself. As for your commissioners I take it for certain that you will choose without change the instrument to complete what he has so well begun. I speak of Simier, of whom having heard all that is laid against him, I swear to you, my dearest, that if he should go out of my life, I see no occasion for his exile. It is true that I know too much indignity used against your person by those who make the people believe that you are so arrogant and so inconstant that they can easily make us withdraw our favour from our dearest when they have us to themselves. And at convenient time I shall not fail to show you to their disgrace who were the authors of it. See where the love that I bear you carries me to make me act contrary to my nature (quite awry from those who fish in troubled waters) to thrust myself in another man's actions. Notwithstanding I cannot refrain from begging you, with hands clasped, to remember that we other princes, holding ourselves in high places, are sought by the testimonies of several heads, amongst whom the greater part accuse us, as our favours are bound by slender threads which make them fear for their favour, amongst whom I wish you to be exempt. Behold, Monsieur, the foolishness of my understanding, who write to you of this matter in hope of a good answer, weighing the place in which you hold us with the company which is there. We poor inhabitants of a barbarous island are not willing to appear for judgment where such subtle judges of our comprehension hold so high a place in the seat of our favour. But appealing to Monsieur alone and not divided, I shall not cease from my suit, even if you should condemn me to the strapado. I shall not add gloss to this text, assuring myself that you understand it only too well. And finally I ask you to pardon this troublesome letter, and to receive my humblest thanks for the offer that

62. *Francis, Duke of Anjou and Duke of Alençon, one of Elizabeth's more favoured suitors, nicknamed 'her frog' in her amused and amusing letters.*

you make me to determine Simier's case as shall seem best to me, assuring you that I have never cared to give you advice which will betray your honour; I will die sooner. I am not partial to him that I forget you, and if there was any infidelity to you of which for my part I have any proof, he is but a stranger to me with whom I have nothing to do, as the Creator knows, Whom I pray grant you a hundred years of life, with my most affectionate commendations. *Postscript.* – I beg you send your good pleasure by this bearer who will return in haste.

Elizabeth to Francis, Duke of Anjou, May 1581

Monsieur, I see well that conjurations are both spiritual and diabolic, first of all because they accomplish much in the eyes of the credulous. I doubt not that you will remember how in your last letter it pleased you to charge me by all the affection that you avowed of old that I would give you a final answer for the direction of the commissioners, and that if the time seemed not convenient, then I should defer it. But to this hour I feel myself so bound by the charm which you lay on me that I cannot persuade myself other than that the Holy Spirit this Pentecost has inspired me to obey your desires, having shown me a rare constancy and affection so signal, which gives me hope that all good fortune will follow so noble a beginning; and for that, if it please you to give order, your deputies can hold themselves ready to come at the time which you think most convenient, considering the time of the year, which seems to me very hot, for an assembly so great as our parliament requires. But I refer all to your good judgment, postponing all impeachments, and stopping my ears to the Sirens that by fair persuasions of my own advantage have somewhat retarded the marriage, considering my age, which could easily make me believe, if there were no other reason, that this conclusion would be very convenient for me. But persuading myself that your denying spirit and understanding, so settled, assures me that you would not willingly buy repentance so dearly, without (not having had so long a time to think of it) well weighing your inclination to perpetuate so good an affection as you have to this present continued, putting entirely on one side my fault; nevertheless, in the name of God, I am resolved to end my days with this sole desire, that you think of me always as I plan to be, drawing no other aim but to be pleasing to you. If the argument of this writing be worthy to plead my excuse, I beg you to hear it, and not to impute it to a lack of goodwill, but rather to some other occasion appertaining to your present knowledge, but very proper for me to know. For the rest, it will please you to incline your ear a little to this bearer, who will tell you from my part certain other matters, from which you will have no need to doubt that you have been negligent in this affair. You know that I am dedicated to your service as you have put me in your obligation. It is time to finish these uneven lines which keep you from your affairs, praying the Creator to keep you in His holy keeping, having trusted myself very cordially in your hands.

Your very assured as well as obliged,
E L I Z A B E T H R.

Elizabeth to Robert Dudley, Earl of Leicester, 19 July 1586

A personal letter to her long-standing favourite whom she nicknamed 'Two Eyes', written ōō.

Rob, I am afraid you will suppose by my wandering writings that a mid-summer moon hath taken large possession of my brains this month, but you must needs take things as they come in my head, though order be left behind me. When I remember your request to have a discreet and honest man that may carry my mind and see how all goes there, I have chosen this bearer, whom you know and have made good trial of. I have fraught him full of my conceits of those country matters, and imparted what way I mind to take, and what is fit for you to use. I am sure you can credit him, and so I will be short with these few notes. First, that Count Maurice and Count Hollocke find themselves trusted of you, esteemed of me and to be carefully regarded if ever peace should happen, and of that assure them on my word that yet never deceived any. And for Norris and other captains that voluntarily without commandment have many years ventured their lives and won our nation honour and themselves fame, [let them] be not discouraged by any means, neither by new-come men nor by old trained soldiers elsewhere. If there be fault in using of soldiers or making of profit by them, let them hear of

63. *A charming political allegory, painted after a pantomime in Paris in 1579. The cow represents The Nether-lands: Philip of Spain is the burden on its back, the Duke of Alva (Spanish Commander in The Netherlands) milks it, Elizabeth feeds it (i.e. with troops and subsidies), while the Duke of Anjou has the thankless task of holding its tail.*

it without open shame and doubt not but I will chasten them therefor. It frets me not a little that the poor soldiers that hourly venture life should want their due, that well deserve rather reward: and look in whom the fault may duly be proved, let them smart therefore. And if the treasurer be found untrue or negli-gent, according to desert he shall be used; though you know my old wont, that love not to discharge from office without desert; God forbid. I pray you let this bearer know what may be learned herein; and for this treasure I have joined Sir Thomas Shirley to see all this money discharged in due sort where it needeth and behoveth. Now will I end that do imagine I talk still with you, and there-fore loathly say farewell, oo, though ever I pray God bless you from all harm and save you from all foes, with my million and legion of thanks for all your pains and cares. As you know, ever the same. E.R.

Elizabeth to Mary, Queen of Scots, October 1586

Mary, Queen of Scots, was brought to trial at Fotheringhay on 12 October 1586.

You have in various ways and manners attempted to take my life and to bring my kingdom to destruction by bloodshed. I have never proceeded so harshly against you, but have, on the contrary, protected and maintained you like myself. These treasons will be proved to you and all made manifest. Yet it is my will, that you answer the nobles and peers of the kingdom as if I were myself present. I therefore require, charge, and command that you make answer for I have been well informed of your arrogance.

Act plainly without reserve, and you will sooner be able to obtain favour of me.

ELIZABETH

Elizabeth to James VI of Scotland, 14 February 1587

Mary was found guilty, but Elizabeth wavered over the signature of the death warrant. When she heard that the execution had been carried out on 8 February, she wrote a letter of seemingly genuine emotion to Mary's son.

My dear Brother, I would you knew (though not felt) the extreme dolour that overwhelms my mind, for that miserable accident which (far contrary to my

64. *The execution of Mary, Queen of Scots.*

meaning) hath befallen. I have now sent this kinsman of mine, whom ere now it hath pleased you to favour, to instruct you truly of that which is too irksome for my pen to tell you. I beseech you that as God and many more know, how innocent I am in this case: so you will believe me, that if I had bid aught I would have bid by it. I am not so base minded that fear of any living creature or prince should make me afraid to do that were just; or done, to deny the same. I am not of so base a lineage, nor carry so vile a mind. But, as not to disguise, fits not a king, so will I never dissemble my actions, but cause them show even as I meant them. Thus assuring yourself of me, that as I know this was deserved, yet if I had meant it I would never lay it on others' shoulders; no more will I not damnify myself that thought it not.

The circumstance it may please you to have of this bearer. And for your part, think you have not in the world a more loving kinswoman, nor a more dear friend than myself; nor any that will watch more carefully to preserve you and your estate. And who shall otherwise persuade you, judge them more partial to others than you. And thus in haste I leave to trouble you: beseeching God to send you a long reign. The 14th of February, 1587.

Your most assured loving sister and cousin,
ELIZAB. R.

65. *An interesting face: the reserved, ruminative image of a strange and devious man – James VI of Scotland, son of Mary, Queen of Scots, and eventually heir to Elizabeth's throne.*

Elizabeth to Robert Devereux, Earl of Essex, May 1596

Elizabeth's last favourite was executed in 1601 following his ill-planned and totally abortive attempt at a coup. This letter was sent just before his expedition to Cadiz, accompanying a prayer she wrote for its success.

I make this humble bill of requests to Him that all makes and does, that with His benign hand He will shadow you so, as all harm may light beside you, and all that may be best hap to your share; that your return may make you better, and me gladder. Let your companion, my most faithful Charles, be sure that his name is not left out in this petition. God bless you both, as I would be if I were there, which, whether I wish or not, He alone doth know.

Elizabeth to Lady Norris, 22 September 1597

Written in her own hand to comfort Lady Norris after her son, Sir John Norris, had been killed on campaign in Ireland.

Mine own Crow, harm not thyself for bootless help; but show a good example to comfort your dolorous yokefellow.

Although we have deferred long to represent unto you our grieved thoughts, because we liked full ill to yield you the first reflection of misfortune, whom we have always sought to cherish and comfort; yet, knowing now that necessity must bring it to your ears, and nature consequently must move both grief and passions in your heart, we resolved no longer to smother either our care for your sorrow, or the sympathy of our grief for his love, wherein, if it be true that society in sorrow works diminution, we do assure you, by this true messenger of our mind, that nature can have stirred no more dolorous affection in you as a mother for a dear son, than gratefulness and memory of his services past hath wrought in us, his sovereign, apprehension of our miss of so worthy a servant. But now that Nature's common work is done, and he that was born to die hath paid his tribute, let that Christian discretion stay the flux of your immoderate grieving, which hath instructed you both by example and knowledge, that nothing of this kind hath happened but by God's divine Providence. And let these lines from your gracious and loving sovereign serve to assure you, that there shall ever appear the lively characters of you and yours that are left, in valuing all their faithful and honest endeavours. More at this time we will not write of this unsilent subject; but have dispatched this gentleman to visit both your lord and you, to condole with you the true sense of your love; and to pray you that the world may see, that what time cureth in weak minds, that discretion and moderation helpeth in you in this accident, where there is so just cause to demonstrate true patience and moderation.

Given at our Manor of Richmond, the 22nd of September, 1597.

66. *The flamboyant bu* *erratic favourite of* *Elizabeth's declining ye* *the Earl of Essex. The* *bitter effect on the Que* *of Essex's rebellion is* *graphically attested by* *Sir John Harington.*

Mr Fenton to Sir John Harington, 23 May 1597

Sir John Harington, the queen's godson, was a wit, scholar, courtier and royal servant. His intimate knowledge of the queen and her Court gives a special significance to the descriptions recorded in his correspondence.

Most respected Friend,

It seemeth marvellous that our gracious queen hath so much annoyance from her most bounden servants; I verily think her highness cannot demand what is not due from any of her subjects. Her own love hath so wrought on us all, that the heart must be evil that doth pay her its small duty so grudgingly as some have done of late. I have not seen her highness, save twice, since Easter last, both of which times she spake vehemently and with great wrath of her servant, the Lady Marie Howard, forasmuch as she had refused to bear her mantle at the hour her highness is wont to air in the garden, and on small rebuke did vent such unseemly answer as did breed much choler in her mistress. Again, on other occasion, she was not ready to carry the cup of grace during the dinner in the privy-chamber, nor was she attending at the hour of her majesty's going to prayer. All which doth now so disquiet her highness, that she swore she would no more show her any countenance, but out with all such ungracious flouting wenches; because, forsooth, she hath much favour and marks of love from the young earl, which is not so pleasing to the queen, who doth still much exhort all her women to remain in virgin state as much as may be. I adventured to say, as far as discretion did go, in defence of our friend; and did urge much in behalf of youth and enticing love, which did often abate of right measures in fair ladies; and moreover related whatever might appease the queen, touching the confession of her great kindness to her sister Jane before her marriage; all which did nothing soothe her highness' anger, saying, 'I have made her my servant, and she will now make herself my mistress; but in good faith, William, she shall not, and so tell her'. In short, pity doth move me to save this lady, and would beg such suit to the queen from you and your friends, as may win her favour to spare her on future amendment. If you could speak to Mr Bellot to urge the Lord Treasurer on this matter, it might not be to good purpose, when a better time doth offer to move the queen than I had; for words then were to no avail, though as discreetly brought as I was able. It might not be amiss to talk to this poor young lady to be more dutiful, and not absent at meals or prayers;

to bear her highness' mantle and other furniture, even more than all the rest of the servants; to make ample amends by future diligence; and always to go first in the morning to her highness' chamber, forasmuch as such kindness will much prevail to turn away all former displeasure. She must not entertain my lord the earl, in any conversation, but shun his company; and moreover be less careful in attiring her own person, for this seemeth as done more to win the earl, than her mistress' good will.

Such, and other advice, as you and other friends are more able to give on these matters, may prevent all other extreme proceeding, especially if it be urged by my Lord Treasurer, in assurance of her good behaviour. If we consider the favours showed her family, there is ground for ill humour in the queen, who doth not now bear with such composed spirit as she was wont; but, since the Irish affairs, seemeth more forward than commonly she used to bear herself toward her women, nor doth she hold them in discourse with such familiar matter, but often chides for small neglects; in such wise, as to make these fair maids often cry and bewail in piteous sort, as I am told by my sister Elizabeth.

Pray observe secrecy in discovering my good will, when you speak to Mr Bellot, or write to the Lord Treasurer; as it is not safe to be too meddling in such matters. Commend me to your Lady Mall, not forgetting her brothers and children. And now in all love I hie to mine office and duty, remaining.

Sir John Harington to Sir Hugh Portman, October 1601

My honoured Friend,
I humbly thank you for that venison I did not eat, but my wife did it much commendation. For six weeks I left my oxen and sheep, and ventured to Court, where I find many leankinded beasts, and some not unhorned. Much was my comfort in being well received, notwithstanding it is an ill hour for seeing the queen. The madcaps are all in riot, and much evil threatened. In good sooth I feared her majesty more than the rebel Tyrone, and wished I had never received my Lord of Essex's honour of knighthood. She is quite disfavoured, and unattired, and these troubles waste her much. She disregarded every costly cover that came to the table, and taken little but manchet and succory potage. Every new message from the city does disturb her, and

she frowns on all the ladies. I had a sharp message from her brought by my
Lord Buckhurst, namely thus, 'Go tell that witty fellow, my godson, to get
home; it is no season now to fool it here'. I liked this as little as she doth my
knighthood, so took to my boots and returned to the plough in bad weather.
I must not say much, even by this trusty and sure messenger; but the many
evil plots and designs have overcome all her highness' sweet temper. She
walks much in her privy chamber, and stamps with her feet at ill news, and
thrusts her rusty sword at times into the arras in great rage. My Lord Buckhurst is much with her, and few else since the city business; but the dangers
are over, and yet she always keeps a sword by her table. I obtained a short
audience at my first coming to Court, when her highness told me, 'If ill
counsel had brought me so far from home, she wish'd Heaven might mar
that fortune which she had mended'. I made my peace in this point, and will
not leave my poor castle of Kelston, for fear of finding a worse elsewhere,
as others have done. I will eat Aldborne rabbits, and get fish (as you
recommend) from the man at Curry-Rival; and get partridge and hares when
I can, and my venison where I can; and leave all great matters to those that
like them better than myself. Commend me to your lady and all other ladies
that ever heard of me. Your books are safe, and I am in liking to get Erasmus
for your entertainment.

Sir John Harington,
'witty fellow' whose
rs give a vivid picture of
igeing Queen.

Sir John Harington to his wife, December 1602

Sweet Mall,

I herewith send thee, what I would God none did know, some ill bodings of the realm and its welfare. Our dear queen, my royal godmother, and this state's natural mother, doth now bear show of human infirmity, too fast for that evil which we shall get by her death, and too slow for that good which she shall get by her releasement from pains and misery.

Dear Mall, how shall I speak what I have seen, or what I have felt? Thy good silence in these matters emboldens my pen. For, thanks to the sweet god of silence! thy lips do not wanton out of discretion's path, like the many gossiping dames we could name, who lose their husband's fast hold in good friends, rather than hold fast their own tongues. Now I will trust thee with great assurance, and whilst thou dost brood over thy young ones in the chamber, thou shalt read the doings of grieving mate in the court.

I find some less mindful of what they are soon to lose, than of what they may perchance hereafter get. Now, on my own part, I cannot blot from my memory's table, the goodness of our sovereign lady to me, even (I will say) before born; her affection to my mother who waited in privy chamber, her bettering the state of my father's fortune (which I have, alas! so much worsted), her watchings over my youth, her liking to my free speech, and admiration of my little learning and poesy, which I did so much cultivate on her command, have rooted such love, such dutiful remembrance of her princely virtues, that to turn askance from her condition with tearless eyes, would stain and foul the spring and fount of gratitude.

It was not many days since I was bidden to her presence. I blest the happy moment; and found her in most pitiable state. She bade the archbishop ask me if I had seen Tyrone? I replied, with reverence, that 'I had seen him with the Lord Deputy'. She looked up, with much choler and grief in her countenance, and said, 'Oh, now it mindeth me that you was one who saw this man elsewhere': and hereat, she dropped a tear, and smote her bosom. She held in her hand a golden cup, which she often put to her lips; but, in sooth, her heart seemeth too full to lack more filling. This sight moved me to think on what past in Ireland; and I trust she did not less think on some who were busier there than myself. She gave me a message to the Lord Deputy; and bade me come to the chamber at seven o'clock. Hereat some who were about her did marvel, and I do not hold so high place as those she did not choose to do her commands. Dear Mall, if I get no profit, I shall get some envy, and this business may turn to some account with the Lord Deputy. Her majesty enquired of some matters which I had written; and as she was pleased to note my fanciful brain, I was not unheedful to feed her humour, and read some verses, whereat she smiled once, and was pleased to say; – 'When thou dost feel creeping time at your gate, these folleries will please thee less; I am past my relish for such matters; thou seest my bodily meat doth not suit me well; I have eaten but one ill tasted cake since yesternight'. She rated most grievously, at noon, at some who minded not to bring up certain matters of account. Several men have been sent to, and when ready at hand, her highness hath dismissed in anger; but who, dearest Mall, shall say, that 'your highness hath forgotten'.

Sir John Harington to Mr Robert Markham, 1606

My good Cousin,

Herewith you will have my journal with our history, during our march against the Irish rebels. I did not intend any eyes should have seen this discourse, but my own children's; yet, alas! it happened otherwise: for the queen did so ask, and, I may say, demand my account, that I could not withhold showing it; and I, even now, almost tremble to rehearse her highness' displeasure hereat. She swore, 'By God's Son, we were all idle knaves, and the Lord Deputy worse, for wasting our time and her commands, in such wise as my journal doth write of'. I could have told her highness of such difficulties, straits, and annoyance, as did not appear therein to her eyes; nor, I found, could not be brought to her ear; for her choler did out-run all reason, though I did meet it at a second hand. For what show she gave at first to my Lord Deputy, at his return, was far more grievous, as will appear in good time. I marvel to think what strange humours do conspire to patch up the natures of some minds. The elements do seem to strive which shall conquer and rise above the other. In good sooth, our late queen did enfold them all together. I bless her memory, for all her goodness to me and my family; and now will I show you what strange temperament she did some-time put forth. Her mind was oftime like the gentle air in a summer's morn; 'twas sweet and refreshing to all around her. Her speech did win all affections, and her subjects did try to show all love to her commands; for she would say, 'her state did require her to command, what she knew her people would willingly do from their own love to her'. Here-in did she show her wisdom fully: for who did choose to lose her confidence; or who would withhold a show of love and obedience, when their sovereign said it was their own choice, and not her compulsion? Surely she did play well her tables to gain obedience thus without constraint: again, she could put forth such alterations, when obedience was lacking, as left no doubtings whose daughter she was. I say this was plain on the Lord Deputy's coming home, when I did come into her presence; she chaffed much, walked fastly to and fro, looked with discomposure in her visage; and, I remember, she catched my girdle when I knelt to her, and swore, 'By God's Son I am no queen; that man is above me; – Who gave him command to come here so soon? I did send him on other business'. It was long before more gracious discourse did fall to my hearing; but I was then put out of my trouble, and bid 'Go home'. I did not stay to be bidden twice; if all the Irish rebels had been at my heels, I should not have had better speed, for I did now flee from one whom I both loved and feared too.

Her highness was wont to sooth her ruffled temper with reading every morning, when she had been stirred to passion at the Council, or other matters had overthrown her gracious disposition. She did much admire Seneca's wholesome advisings, when the soul's quiet was flown away; and I saw much of her translating thereof. By art and nature together so blended, it was difficult to find her right humour at any time. Her wisest men and best counsellors were oft sore troubled to know her will in matters of state: so covertly did she pass her judgment, as seemed to leave all to their discreet management: and, when the business did turn to better advantage, she did most cunningly commit the good issue to her own honour and understanding; but, when ought fell out contrary to her will and intent, the Council were in great strait to defend their own acting and not blemish the queen's good judgment. Herein her wise men did oft lack more wisdom; and the Lord Treasurer would oft shed a plenty of tears on any miscarriage, well knowing the difficult part was, not so much to mend the matter itself, as his mistress's humour: and yet he did most share her favour and good will; and to his opinion she would oft-time submit her own pleasure in great matters. She did keep him till late at night, in discoursing alone, and then call out another at his departure, and try the depth of all around her sometime. Walsingham had his turn, and each displayed their wit in private.

On the morrow, every one did come forth in her presence and discourse at large; and, if any had dissembled with her, or stood not well to her advisings before she did not let it go unheeded, and sometimes not unpunished. Sir Christopher Hatton was wont to say, 'The queen did fish for men's souls, and had so sweet a bait, that no one could escape her network'. In truth, I am sure her speech was such, as none could refuse to take delight in when forwardness did not stand in the way. I have seen her smile, sooth with great semblance of good liking to all around, and cause every one to open his most inward thought to her; when, on a sudden, she would ponder in private on what had passed, write down all their opinions, draw them out as occasion required, and sometime disprove to their faces what had been delivered a month before. Hence she knew one's part, and by thus fishing, as Hatton said, she caught many poor fish, who little knew what snare was laid for them.

I will now tell you more of her majesty's discretion and wonder working to those about her, touching their minds and opinions. She did oft ask the ladies around her chamber if they loved to think of marriage? And the wise ones did conceal well their liking hereto; as knowing the queen's judgment in this matter. Sir Matthew Arundel's fair cousin, not knowing so deeply as her fellows, was asked one day hereof, and simply said – 'She had thought much about marriage, if her father did consent to the man she loved' – 'You seem honest, i'faith', said the queen; 'I will sue for you to your father' – The damsel was not displeased hereat; and, when Sir Robert came to court the queen asked him hereon, and pressed his consenting, if the match was discreet. Sir Robert, much astounded at this news, said – 'He never heard his daughter had liking to any man, and wanted to gain knowledge of her affection; but would give free consent to what was most pleasing to her Highness' will and advice'. – 'Then I will do the rest'; saith the queen. The lady was called in, and the queen told her father had given his free consent. 'Then', replied the lady, 'I shall be happy, and please your grace.' – 'So thou shalt; but not to be a fool and marry. I have his consent given to me, and I vow thou shalt never get it into thy possession: so, go to thy business. I see thou art a bold one, to own thy foolishness so readily'.

I could relate many pleasant tales of her majesty's outwitting the wittiest ones; for few knew how to aim their shaft against her cunning. We did all love her, for she said she loved us, and much wisdom she showed in this matter. She did well temper herself towards all at home, and put at variance those abroad; by which means she had more quit than her neighbours. I need not praise her frugality; but I will tell a story that fell out when I was a boy. She did love a rich clothing, but often chide those that bought more finery than became their state. It happened that Lady M. Howard was possessed of a rich border, powdered with gold and pearl, and a velvet suit belonging thereto, which moved many to envy; nor did it please the queen, who thought it exceeded her own. One day the queen did send privately, and got the lady's rich vesture, which she put on herself, and came forth the chamber among the ladies; the kirtle and border was far too short for her majesty's height; and she asked every one, 'How they liked her new-fancied suit'? At length, she asked the owner herself, 'If it was not made too short and ill-becoming'? which the poor lady did presently consent to. 'Why then, if it become not me, as being too short, I am minded it shall never become thee, as being too fine; so it fitteth neither well'. This sharp rebuke abashed the lady, and she never adorned her herewith any more. I believe the vestment was laid up till after the queen's death.

As I did bear so much love toward her majesty, I know not well how to stop my tales of her virtues, and sometimes her faults, for *nemo nascitur sine —* saith the poet; but even her errors did seem great marks of surprising endowments. When she smiled, it was a pure sunshine, that every one did choose to bask in, if they could; but anon came a storm from a sudden gathering of clouds, and the thunder fell in wondrous manner on all alike. I never did

The Chariott dràwne by foure Horses vpon which Ch[e] stood the Coffin conered w:th purple Veluett and vp[on] that the representation. The Canapy borne by six Knig[hts]

find greater show of understanding and learning, than she was blessed with; and whoever liveth longer than I can, will look back and become *laudator temporis acti*. Yet too, will I praise the present times, or I should be unmindful of many favours received from many hands.

Now will I try to stop, and give your patience a breathing-time from my history; but the subject of the letter will excuse my tedious reciting. I write from wonder and affection. I have now passed my storms, and wish for a quiet harbour to lay up my bark; for I grow old and infirm. I see few friends, and hope I have no enemies. So now adieu, good cousin, and read my tale which I penned of our marches, ambuscades, culverins, and such-like matters; which if it give you no more pleasure in the reading than it did me in the enduring, I must think it a sorry tale truly.

68. *A contemporary sketch of the passing of Queen Elizabeth's funeral cortège: symbolically, perhaps, the passing of the Tudor era.*

ACKNOWLEDGEMENTS

The editor's thanks are due to Gila Curtis who helped him at all stages of the book's preparation and to Andra Nelki for collecting the pictures. The publishers would like to thank those listed below for permission to reproduce the illustrations indicated, or for supplying photographic material.

Her Majesty the Queen 5, 19, 40, 47; Ashmolean Museum, Oxford 15, 20, 41; Duke of Bedford 45; Bodleian Library, Oxford 54; British Museum 13, 17, 22, 24, 25, 27, 30, 35, 38, 39, 43, 49, 61, 68; Duke of Buccleuch and Queensberry 32; Archbishop of Canterbury 50; College of Arms 34; Viscount de L'Isle 48; Mrs M. E. Dent-Brocklehurst 2; Department of the Environment 9, 10; Erlangen Universitätsbibliothek 6; Fitzwilliam Museum, Cambridge 14; John R. Freeman & Co. Ltd 48, 50; Giraudon, Paris 8, 16, 21, 23, 55, 62; Isabella Stewart Gardner Museum, Boston 46; Earl of Jersey 66; Kunsthistorisches Museum, Vienna 11, 21; Musée Condé, Chantilly 8, 16, 62; Musée du Louvre, Paris 23; National Portrait Gallery 3, 12, 28, 36, 42, 56, 59, 67; Nationalmuseum, Stockholm 53; Oeffentlichen Kunstammlung, Basle 31; Pinacoteca Nazionale, Siena 55; Public Record Office 7, 51; St John's College, Cambridge 4; Brigadier D. S. Schreiber 63; Science Museum 37; Scottish National Portrait Gallery 64, 65; Society of Antiquaries, London 33, 44; Staatliche Kunstammlungen, Kassel 57; Times Newspapers Limited 18; Victoria and Albert Museum 26, 29, 52, 58, 60; Walker Art Gallery, Liverpool 1.